The Illustrated World

Atlas

Dr. Alisdair Rogers

CRABTREE
Publishing Company

The Illustrated World Atlas

Crabtree Publishing Company

PMB 59051
350 Fifth Avenue
59th Floor
New York
N.Y. 10118

616 Welland Avenue,
St. Catharines,
Ontario
Canada ON L2M 5V6

Designed by: Sally Boothroyd, Nick Leggett
Edited by: Neil Morris, Vicky Egan
Crabtree editors: Virginia Mainprize, Ellen Rodger
Maps by: Julian Baker
Illustrations by: John Downes, Stuart Lafford, Stephen Lings, Jane Pickering, Chris Rothero, Eric Rowe, and Sarah Smith (Linden Artists); Mike Bell (Specs Art); Tim Haywood

Produced by **Alligator Books Ltd**
Gadd House
Arcadia Avenue
London N3 2JU
United Kingdom

Cataloging-in-Publication Data
Rogers, Alisdair.
 The illustrated world atlas .-- --Rev. ed.
  p. cm.
"Copyright 1998 Andromeda Children's Books, updated Crabtree edition published 2005"--T.p. verso
Includes index.
ISBN-13: 978-0-7787-0040-1 (pbk.) – ISBN-10: 0-7787-0040-2 (pbk.)
1. Children's atlases. I. Crabtree Publishing Company. II. Title.

G1021.R69 2005
912--dc22

2005045001

Contents

How to use this atlas

This atlas divides the world up into 15 regions. Some of the regions, such as Canada, are made up of just one country. But most of them, such as Africa, include a number of countries. On the map on the right, each region is shown in a different color so that you can see at a glance which countries are in each region. Some small islands, not shown on the regional maps in the atlas, have also been named here. If you want to find a particular country, city, river, mountain, or island on one of the maps in this atlas, first look up the name of the place in the gazetteer and index at the back of the book. Next to the name of the place you will see a page number and a grid reference of letters and numbers. Turn to the right page, and then use the grid at the edges of the pages to find the place on the map. (On this page, Mexico's grid reference is F8.)

MAPPING THE WORLD

Earth is a round planet, which makes it very difficult to show on the flat pages of an atlas. To overcome this problem, map-makers cut the world up into segments, rather like peeling an orange, and lay the segments out flat. The result is a flat map of the round Earth, such as the one above.

GREENLAND
(DENMARK)

Arctic Circle

U.S.A.

CANADA

ATLANTIC
OCEAN

UNITED
STATES
OF
AMERICA

PACIFIC
OCEAN

AZORES
(PORT.)

BERMUDA
(U.K.)

Tropic of Cancer

HAWAIIAN
ISLANDS
(U.S.A.)

BAHAMAS

CUBA

MEXICO

DOMINICAN
REPUBLIC

CAPE VER

GUATEMALA
EL SALVADOR

BELIZE
HONDURAS
NICARAGUA

GAMBIA
GUINEA
BISSAU

COSTA RICA

PANAMA

VENEZUELA

GUYANA
SURINAME
FRENCH GUIANA
(FR.)

COLOMBIA

Equator

GALÁPAGOS
ISLANDS
(ECUADOR)

ECUADOR

PERU

BRAZIL

BOLIVIA

Tropic of Capricorn

PARAGUAY

CHILE

URUGUAY

ARGENTINA

FALKLAND
ISLANDS
(U.K.)

SOUTH
GEORGIA
(U.K.)

SOUTH
SANDWIC
ISLAND
(U.K.)

Antarctic Circle

CARIBBEAN ISLANDS
(dependencies in *italics*)
1 *TURKS & CAICOS ISLANDS (U.K.)*
2 *CAYMAN ISLANDS (U.K.)*
3 HAITI
4 JAMAICA
5 *PUERTO RICO (U.S.)*
6 *VIRGIN ISLANDS (U.S./U.K.)*
7 *ANGUILLA (UK)*
8 ST KITTS & NEVIS
9 ANTIGUA & BARBUDA
10 *GUADELOUPE (FR.)*
11 *MONTSERRAT (U.K.)*
12 DOMINICA
13 *MARTINIQUE (FR.)*
14 ST LUCIA
15 ST VINCENT & THE GRENADINES
16 GRENADA
17 BARBADOS
18 TRINIDAD & TOBAGO
19 *ARUBA (NETH.)*
20 *NETHERLANDS ANTILLES (NETH.)*

User's Guide

Locator globes show the position of each region in the world.

Data files give essential facts and figures, including population and land area of the region.

National flags of all independent countries in the region are shown at the top of the pages, together with land area and population of each country.

The **compass** points to north, and the scale bar below shows distance in kilometres and miles.

N

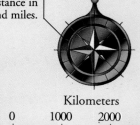

BRUNEI
Area: 2,226 sq. mi.
Population: 372,400

Kilometers
0   1000   2000   3000

0   1000   2000
Miles

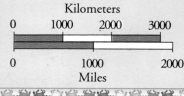

Data file

Area
1,490,354 sq mi./3,859,991 sq km
Population
480 million
ndent countries
31

Ukraine (233,100 sq. mi./603,700 sq km)
Vatican City (0.17 sq. mi./0.44 sq km)
182,431,400)
Spain (4 million)
(15,770

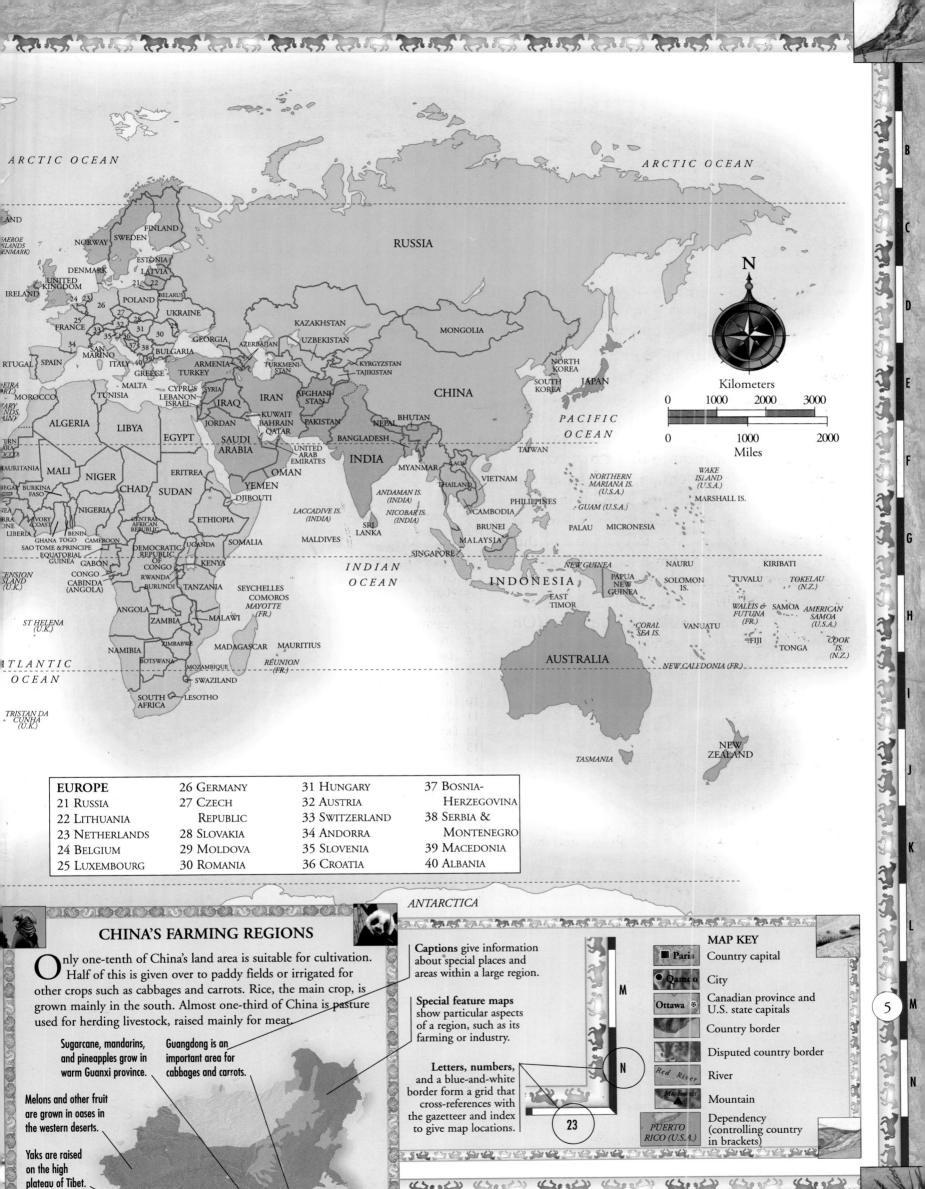

ARCTIC OCEAN

ARCTIC OCEAN

RUSSIA

N

Kilometers

0   1000   2000   3000

0   1000   2000

Miles

FINLAND
NORWAY   SWEDEN
FAEROE
ISLANDS
(DENMARK)
DENMARK
UNITED
KINGDOM   ESTONIA
LATVIA
IRELAND   21   22
POLAND   BELARUS
24 23
26
27   UKRAINE
FRANCE   33   32   31
25
34   35 36   30
SAN   37 38
MARINO   ITALY   40 39
GREECE
PORTUGAL   SPAIN   TURKEY
MADEIRA
(PORT.)
MALTA   CYPRUS
TUNISIA   LEBANON
ISRAEL   SYRIA
CANARY
ISLANDS
(SPAIN)
MOROCCO   JORDAN
ALGERIA   LIBYA   EGYPT
SAUDI
ARABIA
MAURITANIA   MALI   NIGER   CHAD   SUDAN
ERITREA
YEMEN
OMAN
DJIBOUTI
SENEGAL
BURKINA
FASO   NIGERIA
GUINEA
SIERRA
LEONE
LIBERIA   GHANA TOGO   BENIN   CAMEROON
SAO TOME &PRINCIPE
EQUATORIAL
GUINEA   GABON
CENTRAL
AFRICAN
REPUBLIC
UGANDA
ETHIOPIA
SOMALIA
KENYA
ASCENSION
ISLAND
(U.K.)   CONGO
CABINDA
(ANGOLA)
DEMOCRATIC
REPUBLIC
OF
CONGO
RWANDA
BURUNDI   TANZANIA
SEYCHELLES
COMOROS
MAYOTTE
(FR.)
ANGOLA
ST HELENA
(U.K.)   ZAMBIA   MALAWI
ZIMBABWE
NAMIBIA   BOTSWANA   MADAGASCAR   MAURITIUS
RÉUNION
(FR.)
MOZAMBIQUE
TRISTAN DA
CUNHA
(U.K.)   SWAZILAND
SOUTH
AFRICA   LESOTHO

GEORGIA
AZERBAIJAN
ARMENIA
TURKMENI-
STAN
IRAN
IRAQ
KUWAIT
BAHRAIN
QATAR
UNITED
ARAB
EMIRATES
KAZAKHSTAN
UZBEKISTAN
KYRGYZSTAN
TAJIKISTAN
AFGHANI-
STAN
PAKISTAN
INDIA
MONGOLIA
NEPAL   BHUTAN
BANGLADESH
MYANMAR
LAOS
THAILAND
VIETNAM
CHINA
NORTH
KOREA
SOUTH
KOREA
JAPAN
TAIWAN

LACCADIVE IS.
(INDIA)
ANDAMAN IS.
(INDIA)
NICOBAR IS.
(INDIA)
SRI
LANKA
MALDIVES
CAMBODIA
BRUNEI
MALAYSIA
SINGAPORE
PHILIPPINES
NORTHERN
MARIANA IS.
(U.S.A.)
GUAM (U.S.A.)
PALAU   MICRONESIA
WAKE
ISLAND
(U.S.A.)
MARSHALL IS.

INDIAN
OCEAN

PACIFIC
OCEAN

ATLANTIC
OCEAN

INDONESIA
NEW GUINEA
EAST
TIMOR
PAPUA
NEW
GUINEA
SOLOMON
IS.
NAURU
TUVALU
KIRIBATI
TOKELAU
(N.Z.)
WALLIS &
FUTUNA
(FR.)   SAMOA   AMERICAN
SAMOA
(U.S.A.)
CORAL
SEA IS.   VANUATU
FIJI   TONGA
COOK
IS.
(N.Z.)
AUSTRALIA
NEW CALEDONIA (FR.)

TASMANIA
NEW
ZEALAND

ANTARCTICA

EUROPE	26 GERMANY	31 HUNGARY	37 BOSNIA-
21 RUSSIA	27 CZECH	32 AUSTRIA	HERZEGOVINA
22 LITHUANIA	REPUBLIC	33 SWITZERLAND	38 SERBIA &
23 NETHERLANDS	28 SLOVAKIA	34 ANDORRA	MONTENEGRO
24 BELGIUM	29 MOLDOVA	35 SLOVENIA	39 MACEDONIA
25 LUXEMBOURG	30 ROMANIA	36 CROATIA	40 ALBANIA

CHINA'S FARMING REGIONS

Only one-tenth of China's land area is suitable for cultivation. Half of this is given over to paddy fields or irrigated for other crops such as cabbages and carrots. Rice, the main crop, is grown mainly in the south. Almost one-third of China is pasture used for herding livestock, raised mainly for meat.

Sugarcane, mandarins, and pineapples grow in warm Guanxi province.

Guangdong is an important area for cabbages and carrots.

Melons and other fruit are grown in oases in the western deserts.

Yaks are raised on the high plateau of Tibet.

Forest

Herding

Captions give information about special places and areas within a large region.

Special feature maps show particular aspects of a region, such as its farming or industry.

Letters, numbers, and a blue-and-white border form a grid that cross-references with the gazetteer and index to give map locations.

M

N

23

MAP KEY

Paris   Country capital

Qamco   City

Ottawa   Canadian province and U.S. state capitals

Country border

Disputed country border

Red River   River

Mt Everest   Mountain

PUERTO
RICO (U.S.A.)   Dependency (controlling country in brackets)

Our planet in space

The universe contains millions of galaxies, and each one, even the smallest, is made up of millions of stars. One of those millions of stars, in the galaxy called the Milky Way, is our own Sun. All life on earth depends on the sun's energy, which gives light and warmth to humans, animals, and plants. The earth travels around the sun. It takes a year for the earth to go around the sun once; and because the earth is tilted, we have seasons. For example, for the part of the year that the north is nearer the sun than the south, we have northern summers and southern winters. The earth also spins as it travels, giving us night and day.

OUR GALAXY

Astronomers think that there are about 100,000 million galaxies in the universe. Our galaxy, the Milky Way (left), is just one of them. It is spiral shaped, with curved "arms", and is made up of about 100,000 million stars! Our sun is a star on one of its arms. On clear nights, you can see some of the stars in the Milky Way forming a bright band of "milky-coloured" light across the sky.

THE SOLAR SYSTEM

Earth is one of the planets that travel around the star that we call the Sun. These planets, together with their moons and the Sun, make up the solar system. Mercury (1, above) is the closest planet to the Sun, followed by Venus (2), Earth (3), Mars (4), Jupiter (5), Saturn (6), Uranus (7), Neptune (8). Pluto (9) used to be thought of as a planet, but new technology has revealed that is in fact a "dwarf" planet as it does not dominate its neighborhood.

INSIDE THE EARTH

The earth is like a giant ball made up of different layers. The outer layer is called the earth's crust. All the continents and the oceans shown on the maps in this atlas lie on the earth's crust. Movements of huge pieces of the crust, called plates, cause earthquakes. Below the crust is the mantle. Sometimes, the mantle's molten rock, called magma, breaks through cracks in the crust and forms volcanoes. Deeper down, the earth's core is made up of two parts: a liquid outer core and a solid inner core.

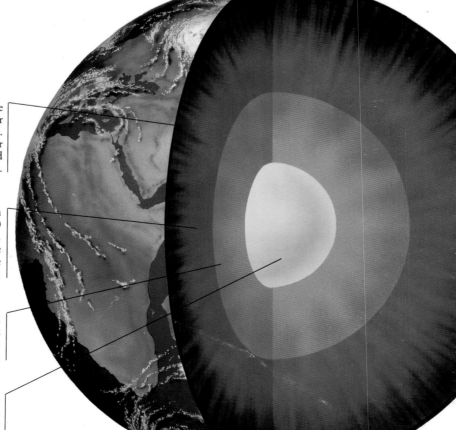

The **crust**, the earth's hard outer layer, is up to 31 mi. (50 km) thick under the oceans and continents.

The **mantle** goes down to a depth of 1,800 mi. (2,900 km). In some places, the hot rocks move very slowly.

The **outer core** is a very hot, thick liquid made of iron and nickel.

The **inner core** is under such pressure that it is a solid mass.

Climate and vegetation

The climate, or typical weather conditions, of a region depends on its location. Regions close to the equator are hottest, and those nearest the poles are coldest. In between there are temperate, or mild, regions. How high a place is above sea level, and how near it is to a coast, also affect its climate. Coastal areas tend to have warmer winters and cooler summers than inland areas. The climate of a place has a major influence on its vegetation, or plant life.

TEMPERATE FOREST

This type of mild-weather forest occurs in North America, Europe and the far east of Asia. It is made up mainly of broadleaf, "deciduous" trees, which means they shed their leaves in the fall. Before they drop, the leaves turn red, orange, yellow, or brown. These temperate forest trees (above) are in the Great Smoky Mountains National Park, Tennessee, U.S.A.

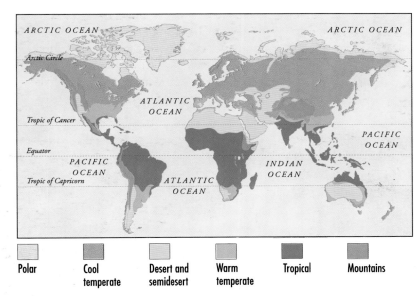

Polar | Cool temperate | Desert and semidesert | Warm temperate | Tropical | Mountains

LANDSCAPES AND CLIMATE

In the tropics, the area between the Tropic of Cancer and the Tropic of Capricorn, there is dense tropical forest, rainfall is over 80 in. (2,000 mm) a year and temperatures average 77° F (25° C). Deserts cover one-seventh of the earth; here it can be over 100° F (37° C) by day, but below freezing at night. In the Arctic polar region there is a treeless tundra landscape of low-growing plants and mosses around the edge of the ice sheets. Farther south, in the cool temperate region, there are vast bands of coniferous forest. These give way to deciduous forest and grassland in the warm temperate region.

TROPICAL RAIN FOREST

In tropical regions near the equator, the climate is hot and wet all year round. These conditions create habitats for more kinds of plants and animals than anywhere else. Tropical rain forests are found in Central and South America, Africa, South East Asia, and northern Australia. The trees often support climbing plants and are home to colorful birds, monkeys, and other animals (right). Huge areas of rain forest are being cut down to provide people with wood for fuel and to create farmland. Conservationists around the world are trying hard to stop the destruction of these important habitats.

DRY SOUTH AMERICA

The Atacama Desert (above), in Chile, is probably the driest place on earth. A squall of rain may strike small parts of it only a few times in a hundred years!

WET SOUTH AMERICA

Tutunendo, in Colombia (above), lies about 1,850 mi. (3,000 km) north of the dry Atacama Desert. It is one of the wettest places in the world!

The world's top five

The world is full of amazing natural and human-made wonders, from mighty rivers that cross continents to cities with more people than the entire population of some countries. All the world's highest mountains are in the same mountain range: the Himalayas, between China, Pakistan, India, Nepal, and Bhutan. Most of the rest of the record features, the largest lakes and islands, for example, are spread out across the world. The world's "top fives" are all shown on the map opposite.

Largest cities
(urban agglomeration)

Tokyo	Japan	35.1 million
Mexico City	Mexico	19.4 million
New York City	United States	18.7 million
São Paulo	Brazil	18.3 million
Mumbai	India	18.1 million

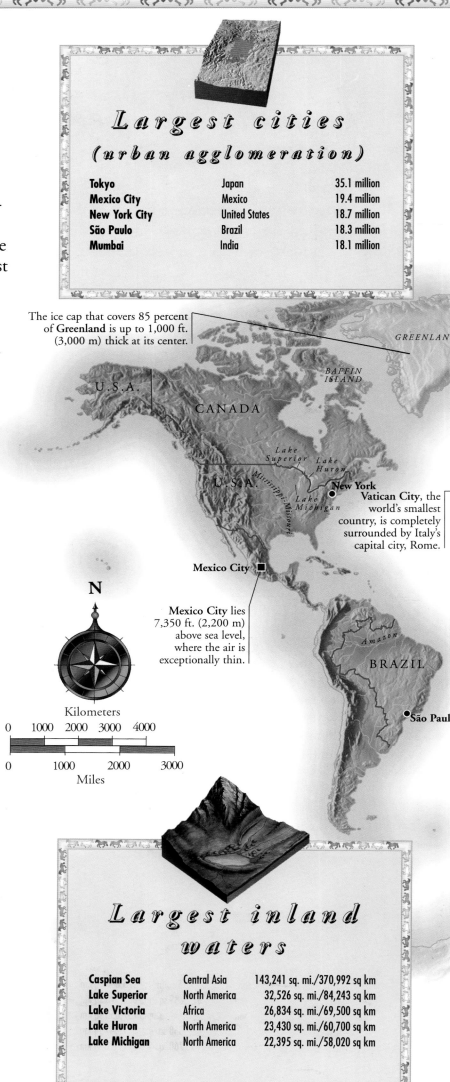

The ice cap that covers 85 percent of **Greenland** is up to 1,000 ft. (3,000 m) thick at its center.

GREENLAND

BAFFIN ISLAND

U.S.A.

CANADA

Lake Superior Lake Huron

U.S.A.

Lake Michigan

Mississippi–Missouri

New York

Vatican City, the world's smallest country, is completely surrounded by Italy's capital city, Rome.

Mexico City

Mexico City lies 7,350 ft. (2,200 m) above sea level, where the air is exceptionally thin.

Amazon

BRAZIL

São Paulo

N

Kilometers

0   1000   2000   3000   4000

0   1000   2000   3000

Miles

Highest mountains

Mount Everest	Nepal/China	29,035 ft./8,850 m
K2	India	28,250 ft./8,611 m
Kanchenjunga	Nepal/India	28,169 ft./8,586 m
Lhotse I	Nepal/China	27,939 ft./8,516 m
Makalu	Nepal/China	27,765 ft./8,462 m

Longest rivers

Nile	Africa	4,160 mi./6,695 km
Amazon	South America	3,969 mi./6,387 km
Mississippi–Missouri	United States	3,896 mi./6,270 km
Yangtze or Chang	China	3,859 mi./6,211 km
Yenisei	Russia	3,449 mi./5,550 km

Largest inland waters

Caspian Sea	Central Asia	143,241 sq. mi./370,992 sq km
Lake Superior	North America	32,526 sq. mi./84,243 sq km
Lake Victoria	Africa	26,834 sq. mi./69,500 sq km
Lake Huron	North America	23,430 sq. mi./60,700 sq km
Lake Michigan	North America	22,395 sq. mi./58,020 sq km

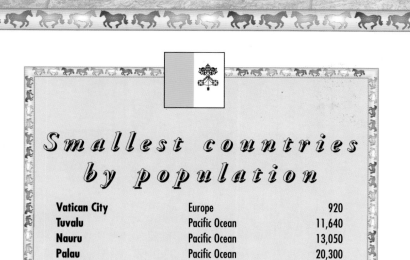

Smallest countries by population

Vatican City	Europe	920
Tuvalu	Pacific Ocean	11,640
Nauru	Pacific Ocean	13,050
Palau	Pacific Ocean	20,300
San Marino	Europe	28,880

Largest countries by population

China	Asia	1,306,313,800
India	Asia	1,080,264,400
U.S.A.	North America	295,734,100
Indonesia	Asia	241,973,900
Brazil	South America	186,112,800

Russia's land area is 11.5 percent of the land area of the world.

The surface of the **Caspian Sea** is 92 ft. (28 m) below sea level.

Mount Everest's height of 29,035 ft. (8,850 m) was first measured in 1852 by a British survey team.

China's present population is more than that of the whole world 150 years ago!

Smallest countries by area

Vatican City	Europe	0.17 sq. mi./0.44 sq km
Monaco	Europe	0.75 sq. mi./1.95 sq km
Nauru	Pacific Ocean	8 sq. mi./21 sq km
Tuvalu	Pacific Ocean	9.27 sq. mi./24 sq km
San Marino	Europe	23.6 sq. mi./61 sq km

Largest islands

Greenland	Arctic Ocean	840,325 sq. mi./2,175,600 sq km
New Guinea	Pacific Ocean	312,085 sq. mi./808,510 sq km
Borneo	Pacific Ocean	292,220 sq. mi./757,050 sq km
Madagascar	Indian Ocean	226,658 sq. mi./587,041 sq km
Baffin Island	Arctic Ocean	183,760 sq. mi./476,070 sq km

Largest countries by area

Russia	Asia	6,592,800 sq. mi./17,075,400 sq km
Canada	North America	3,851,817 sq. mi./9,976,140 sq km
China	Asia	3,676,300 sq. mi./9,526,900 sq km
USA	North America	3,539,243 sq. mi./9,166,600 sq km
Brazil	South America	3,265,076 sq. mi./8,456,508 sq km

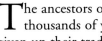

CANADA
Area: 3,851,791 sq. mi.
Population: 32,805,000

Canada
People and places

Canada is a vast land of forests, mountains, plains and lakes. It is the second biggest country in the world: only Russia has a greater land area. The population of nearly 33 million people is very small for such a big country. Canada's original inhabitants include the Inuit and the Native peoples of the First Nations. The Inuit live in remote settlements in the cold north where there are few roads. Most Canadians live in the warmer south, in a narrow band just north of the border with the United States. Here there are big cities such as Toronto, Montréal, and Vancouver. New immigrants from many other countries have added to Canada's culture, which for hundreds of years has linked British and French traditions.

THE INUIT
The ancestors of the Inuit crossed from Siberia thousands of years ago. Today, many Inuit have given up their traditional hunting and fishing life to settle in small northern communities.
♦ *The ancestral home of the Inuit is called Nunavut, meaning "our land".*

ARCTIC OCEAN

Arctic Circle

BEAUFORT SEA

Queen Elizabeth Islands

Banks Island

Victoria Island

BERING SEA

U.S.A. (ALASKA)

• Inuvik
Ft. McPherson

MACKENZIE MOUNTAINS

Mackenzie

YUKON TERRITORY

▲ Mt. Logan

Whitehorse

Great Bear Lake

• Ft. Norman

NORTHWEST TERRITORIES

Yellowknife

Great Slave Lake

PACIFIC OCEAN

ROCKY MOUNTAINS

Peace

QUEEN CHARLOTTE ISLANDS

• Prince Rupert

ALBERTA

Athabasca

N. Saskatchewan

BRITISH COLUMBIA

Edmonton

SASKATCHEWAN

Saskatoon

Vancouver

• Calgary

S. Saskatchewan

Victoria

Regina

Victoria, the capital of British Columbia, is on Vancouver Island. The city of Vancouver is on the mainland.

Canada's border with the United States is the world's longest undefended international boundary.

CANADIAN NATIONAL TOWER
The CN Tower in Toronto was built in 1976. It is 1,814 ft. (553 m) high. Glass-faced elevators take visitors up to two observation decks, one of which has a see-through floor.
♦ *Toronto was founded in 1793. Toronto means "meeting place" in the Huron language.*

FRENCH CANADA
French fur traders and farmers were among the earliest Europeans to settle in Canada. Later, the French and British fought for control of the country, and the British won in 1760. The country was formed in 1867 by an agreement called Confederation. The famous hotel building, called Château Frontenac (right), is in Québec City, the capital of the province of Quebec. Most of the people of Quebec speak French, and today many French Canadians want greater independence.
♦ *Canada has two official languages, English and French.*

RODEO

Rodeos are festivals of cowboy skills. They include competitions for riding bucking broncos, wrestling steers, and racing chuck wagons. The Calgary Stampede (right) is the world's biggest rodeo. It lasts 10 days every July and competitors come from all over North America.

♦ *In calf-roping contests, cowboys lasso a calf and tie three of its legs together. They lose points for being too rough.*

FIRST NATIONS

Canada's First Nations include the Inuit of the north and many aboriginal Native Indian peoples, such as the Ojibwe, the Micmac, the Mohawk, and the Blackfoot. The *Métis* are of mixed aboriginal and French heritage. First Nations people of the Pacific coast made tall totem poles (right), on which they carved images of their supernatural clan ancestors.

♦ *The Blackfoot once hunted buffalo on the plains, and the Huron were farmers in the Great Lakes region.*

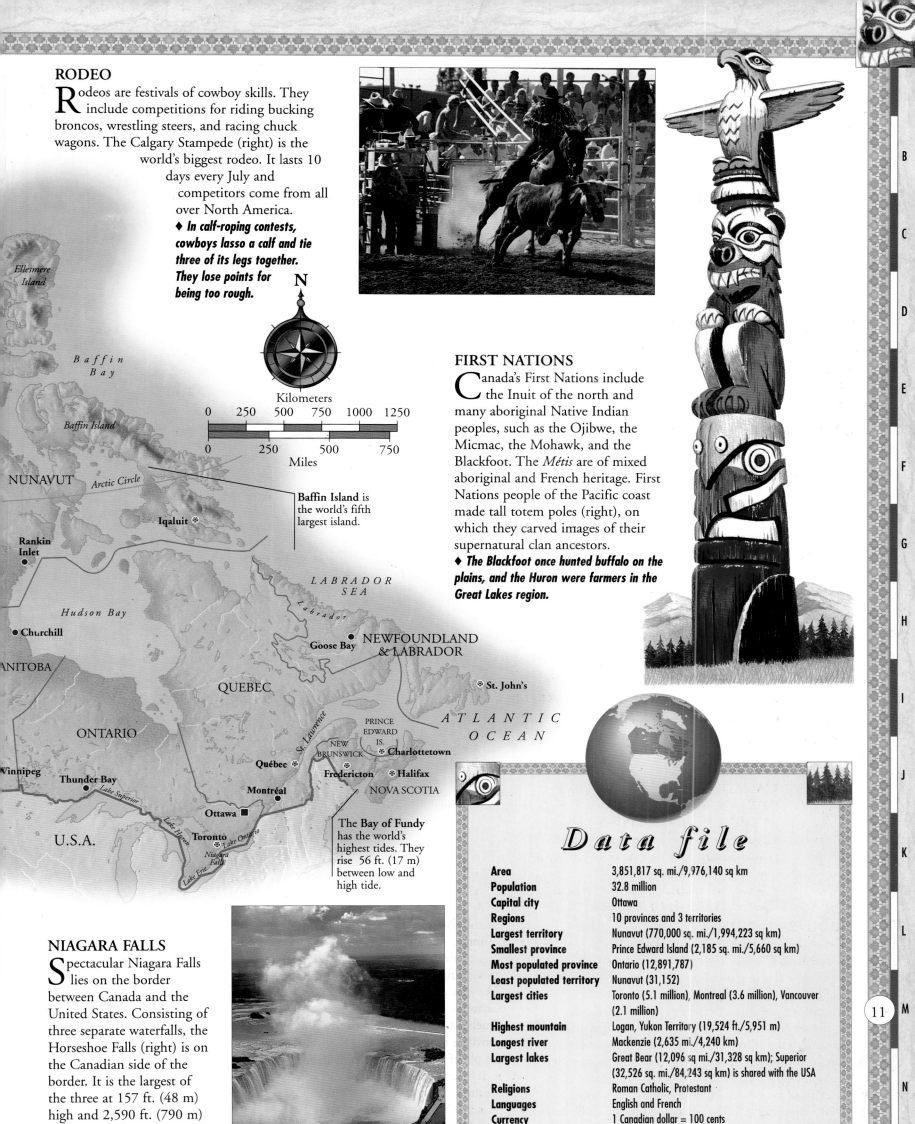

N

Kilometers
0   250   500   750   1000   1250

0   250   500   750
Miles

Baffin Island is the world's fifth largest island.

Ellesmere Island

Baffin Bay

Baffin Island

NUNAVUT   Arctic Circle

Iqaluit ✷

Rankin Inlet ●

Hudson Bay

● Churchill

ANITOBA

LABRADOR SEA

Labrador

Goose Bay ● NEWFOUNDLAND & LABRADOR

✷ St. John's

QUEBEC

ONTARIO

ATLANTIC OCEAN

Winnipeg ●

Thunder Bay ●

Lake Superior

Québec ✷

St. Lawrence

PRINCE EDWARD IS.

NEW BRUNSWICK

✷ Charlottetown

Fredericton ✷   ✷ Halifax

NOVA SCOTIA

Montréal ●

Ottawa ■

Lake Huron

U.S.A.

Toronto ●

Lake Ontario

Niagara Falls

Lake Erie

The **Bay of Fundy** has the world's highest tides. They rise 56 ft. (17 m) between low and high tide.

NIAGARA FALLS

Spectacular Niagara Falls lies on the border between Canada and the United States. Consisting of three separate waterfalls, the Horseshoe Falls (right) is on the Canadian side of the border. It is the largest of the three at 157 ft. (48 m) high and 2,590 ft. (790 m) wide.

♦ *Niagara Falls is one of the greatest hydro-electric power sources in the world.*

Data file

Area	3,851,817 sq. mi./9,976,140 sq km
Population	32.8 million
Capital city	Ottawa
Regions	10 provinces and 3 territories
Largest territory	Nunavut (770,000 sq. mi./1,994,223 sq km)
Smallest province	Prince Edward Island (2,185 sq. mi./5,660 sq km)
Most populated province	Ontario (12,891,787)
Least populated territory	Nunavut (31,152)
Largest cities	Toronto (5.1 million), Montreal (3.6 million), Vancouver (2.1 million)
Highest mountain	Logan, Yukon Territory (19,524 ft./5,951 m)
Longest river	Mackenzie (2,635 mi./4,240 km)
Largest lakes	Great Bear (12,096 sq mi./31,328 sq km); Superior (32,526 sq. mi./84,243 sq km) is shared with the USA
Religions	Roman Catholic, Protestant
Languages	English and French
Currency	1 Canadian dollar = 100 cents

Canada:
Nature, farming and industry

Canada is rich in natural resources such as timber, minerals and oil. Some of these are found in the remote treeless plains of the tundra in the far north. In order to exploit the natural resources, engineers have built long railways, roads and canals for transportation, and huge dams to make electricity. National parks have been set up to protect the local wildlife from disturbance. Caribou live on the tundra, and in the forests there are bears, moose and beavers. Fishing is an important industry along the coasts, and on the central prairies there are huge wheat fields surrounding isolated farmsteads.

TIMBER TRAIN

Canada's farm and forest products have to be moved long distances to factories and cities, or to ports for shipment abroad. Long goods trains, like this one in the Rocky Mountains of British Columbia (above), are used. Two big Canadian rail companies, CP Rail and CN North America, haul over 100,000 million tonnes (98,420 million tons) of freight a year. In the mountains, many tunnels and bridges had to be built to carry the railway track.
♦ *The original Canadian Pacific Railway opened in 1885. It ran all the way from the Atlantic coast to the Pacific coast.*

FISHING BEARS

Brown bears, often called grizzly bears (right), will eat almost anything, including meat, fruit, honey, insects and fish. They live mostly in forested mountain areas where there are fast-flowing rivers. Some catch salmon by grabbing them out of the water as they swim by, some jump in and flip them onto the bank, and others catch them in their jaws as the salmon leap upstream.
♦ *Salmon are born and die in freshwater rivers, but spend half their life in the ocean.*

Snow goose

Caribou

TUNDRA LANDSCAPE

In the vast, flat tundra region of northern Canada, the temperature falls well below freezing in winter. Because the climate is so dry all year there are no trees. The ground is frozen, and only the upper layer thaws in the short summers. Lichens grow on rocks and frozen ground. Only grasses, moss, and some shrubs can grow in the thin layer of soil. In winter many birds and animals migrate south to warmer regions. Herds of caribou may travel more than 600 miles (over 1,000 kilometers) to the Canadian forests, while snow geese fly to the southern United States.
♦ *In winter, caribou use their hooves and antlers to dig through the snow to find lichens and moss to eat.*

Snowshoe hare

PRAIRIE PROVINCES

The prairies are grassland plains that cover much of the provinces of Alberta, Saskatchewan and Manitoba. Rich soils make for huge wheat fields (right). In drier areas there are also vast cattle ranches. The prairies are covered with snow during winter, but in spring a warm wind called the chinook blows off the Rocky Mountains and melts the snow. In the hot summers there can be droughts and fierce dust storms.

♦ *Canada produces 30 million tonnes (29.5 million tons) of wheat a year.*

CHANGING COLOUR

Some Arctic animals change colour from summer to winter to protect themselves from predators. The brown summer coats of Arctic foxes (below) and Arctic hares change to thicker white coats in winter. This helps them to keep warm in the freezing temperatures and also camouflages them against the snowy landscape.

♦ *In winter Arctic foxes have to travel a long way to find food. They hunt for small animals or fish.*

Arctic foxes

MAKING PAPER

Almost half of Canada is covered by forest, and the country's timber industry is very important. Soft woods from British Columbia, Québec, and Ontario is made into paper. Logs are taken to pulp mills (left), where the bark is stripped off in revolving drums and the wood is chipped by machines. It is then ground up or boiled with chemicals and mixed with water to make pulp. Finally, the pulp is strained, dried, and rolled into paper.

♦ *Canadian pulp mills produce a third of the world's newsprint.*

WOLVES OF THE FORESTS

Grey wolves live in woodland and forests right across Canada, including the Rocky Mountains. They live in family groups, which often join together to form packs of more than 20 animals. They may hunt together, helping to bring down large prey such as deer and caribou. On their own they catch rabbits and mice. Each wolf pack has a strict order, and the leading male signals his rank by carrying his tail higher than the others.

♦ *Wolves howl to let their own pack members know where they are, or to warn other packs to keep their distance.*

Ptarmigan

Arctic lemming

UNITED STATES OF AMERICA
Area: 3,539,243 sq. mi.
Population: 295,734,100

United States of America
People and places

The U.S.A is the fourth largest country in the world and the third most populated. No other country has such an enormous political, economic, and cultural influence. Hollywood films and American television programs are watched almost everywhere, and American industries make products used by people all over the world. Other countries have influenced the United States, too. People from every continent have migrated to the U.S.A., bringing their culture and talents to their new homeland.

ON CAPITOL HILL

The Capitol building is in Washington, D.C., the capital of the U.S.A. The U.S. Congress meets there to discuss and vote on new laws.

♦ *The U.S. president lives in the White House, near the Capitol.*

ALASKA

Nicknamed the "Last Frontier," Alaska is a wilderness of high mountains, clear lakes, and huge glaciers. It is separated from the rest of the U.S.A. by Canada.

♦ *Alaska is the biggest of the 50 states. Texas is the second biggest.*

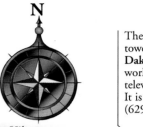

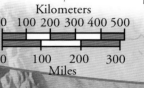

The KVLY-TV tower in **North Dakota** is the world's tallest television tower. It is 2,064 ft. (629 m) high.

HAWAII

This group of volcanic islands lies far from the U.S. mainland, in the Pacific Ocean.

♦ *Hawaii became a U.S. state in 1959.*

Kauai
Oahu
Maui
Honolulu
HAWAII
Mauna Kea
Mauna Loa

Kilometers 0 — 200
Miles 0 — 200

Each American state has its own capital. **Phoenix** is the capital of Arizona.

TREND-SETTERS

Baseball and skateboarding were invented in the United States, and rock music was born there. American fast foods are popular in many countries.

Baseball

♦ *Los Angeles is the film center, and New York City is the center of the fashion business.*

Skateboard

Hamburger and popcorn

Rock guitar

STATUE OF LIBERTY

This landmark stands on its own island in New York Harbor. It was a gift from the people of France, to celebrate the hundredth anniversary of the U.S. Declaration of Independence which was signed in 1776.

♦ *The Statue of Liberty is 148.6 ft. (45.3 m) high.*

RAIN DANCE

The Pueblo people of New Mexico (below) dance in the hope that rain will come and help their crops grow. They have kept up many traditional ways.

♦ *There are about 2.5 million Native Americans in the U.S.A.*

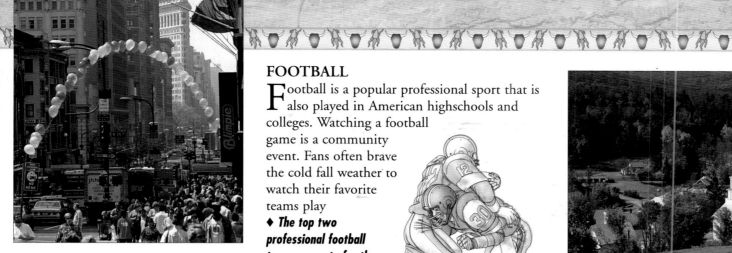

FOOTBALL

Football is a popular professional sport that is also played in American highschools and colleges. Watching a football game is a community event. Fans often brave the cold fall weather to watch their favorite teams play

◆ *The top two professional football teams compete for the annual Super Bowl trophy.*

MIXTURE OF PEOPLE

In New York (above) there are large communities of Puerto Ricans, Italians, Irish, Chinese, and people from many other countries.

◆ *One in twelve Americans was born outside the United States.*

New England is made up of six states: Maine, New Hampshire, Vermont, Massachusetts, Rhode Island and Connecticut.

NEW ENGLAND

The gentle hills and beautiful woods near the northeast coast of the United States reminded many of the early English settlers of home, so they called the region New England. In states such as Vermont (above) and Massachusetts, they founded small towns and villages which they often named after places in England.

◆ *The earliest settlers arrived in New England on a ship called the Mayflower in 1620. They came in search of a new life.*

MINNESOTA
Lake Superior
Duluth
MICHIGAN
argo
Minneapolis
Lake Huron
St. Paul
WISCONSIN
Green Bay
Grand Rapids
Sioux Falls
Milwaukee
Lake Michigan
Lansing
Madison
Rockford
Detroit
Lake Erie
Buffalo
IOWA
Chicago
INDIANA OHIO
Cleveland
Davenport
PENNSYLVANIA
maha Des Moines
Columbus
ILLINOIS
Indianapolis Dayton
Harrisburg
Pittsburgh
coln
Springfield
Cincinnati
Ohio
WEST VIRGINIA
ansas City
St. Louis
Louisville
Frankfort
Charleston
VIRGINIA
ne Topeka
Jefferson City
KENTUCKY
MISSOURI
Wichita
Springfield
Nashville
Raleigh
NORTH CAROLINA
Charlotte
ulsa
TENNESSEE
ARKANSAS
SOUTH CAROLINA
Wilmington
homa City
Memphis
Columbia
Tennessee
Augusta
Little Rock
Atlanta
HOMA
Arkansas
Birmingham
Charleston
allas
MISSISSIPPI ALABAMA
GEORGIA
ATLANTIC OCEAN
Montgomery
ort Worth
LOUISIANA Jackson
Albany
Mobile
Jacksonville
Tallahassee
Baton Rouge
ustin
New Orleans
Orlando
Cape Canaveral
Houston
Tampa
Galveston
FLORIDA
GULF OF MEXICO
Lake Okeechobee
Miami
Everglades
Florida Keys

MAINE
Bangor
Augusta
VERMONT
Montpelier Portland
Concord NEW HAMPSHIRE
Lake Ontario
MASSACHUSETTS
Rochester Albany Boston
Cape Cod
NEW YORK Hartford Providence
RHODE ISLAND
CONNECTICUT
New York
NEW JERSEY
Trenton
Philadelphia
Baltimore Dover
WASHINGTON D.C. Annapolis DELAWARE
MARYLAND
Richmond
Chesapeake Bay
APPALACHIAN MOUNTAINS

MISSISSIPPI STEAMBOAT

The Mississippi River was important in the development of the U.S.A. People and goods could travel along it, from the heart of the country to New Orleans on the Gulf of Mexico. They were carried on steamboats (below), which were powered by a steam-driven revolving paddle wheel.

◆ *The first steamer, called the New Orleans, ran in 1811. Today, most goods are moved along the river in barge convoys.*

Data file

Area	3,539,243 sq. mi./9,166,600 sq km
Population	295.7 million
Number of states	50, plus the District of Columbia
Capital city	Washington, D.C. (District of Columbia)
Largest state	Alaska (586,393 sq. mi./1,518,748 sq km)
Smallest state	Rhode Island (468 sq. mi./1,212 sq km)
Most populated state	California (32,601,000)
Least populated state	Wyoming (484,000)
Largest cities	New York (16.6), Los Angeles (3.9 million)
	Chicago (2.9 million)
Highest mountain	Mount McKinley, Alaska (20,320 ft./6,194 m)
Longest river	Mississippi–Missouri (3,896 mi./6,270 km)
Largest lakes	Michigan (22,395 sq. mi./58,020 sq km); Superior (32,526 sq. mi./84,243 sq km) is shared with Canada
Religions	Protestant, Roman Catholic, Jewish
Languages	English; also a large Spanish-speaking population
Currency	1 US dollar = 100 cents

How places got their names

Chicago	from a Native American word for *place where wild onions grow*
Florida	from the Spanish, meaning *flowery*
Louisiana	after King Louis XIV of France
Missouri	from the name of a Native American tribe

United States of America: *Nature*

The American climate varies from the warmth of tropical Florida and Pacific Hawaii to the cold of Arctic Alaska. There are deserts in Arizona and California, and forests in the Rocky and Appalachian Mountains. The plains across the heart of the United States are drained by the Mississippi river and its tributaries, including the Missouri. Between the USA and Canada are the five Great Lakes, created when glaciers moved north thousands of years ago. Many different animals live in these different habitats. Wolves, bears, and mountain lions live in the forests, buffaloes and pronghorns roam across the plains, and there are alligators in the southern swamps.

RUGGED COAST

The Santa Lucia mountain range rises straight from the Pacific Ocean on the California coast south of San Francisco.

♦ *You can often see seals and whales from the rocky cliffs.*

Pronghorn

Buffalo

Scarlet mallow

Prairie dog

MONUMENT VALLEY

This breathtaking natural landscape lies high on the Colorado plateau, on the borders of Utah and Arizona. Because the ancient sandstone is harder than the surrounding rocks, it has worn away less. This has left towering pillars and buttes, which glow red and orange in the sun. One rock tower is a volcanic plug, a mass of hard lava left behind when the rest of the volcano wore away.

♦ *The famous film director John Ford shot classic "Westerns" such as* Stagecoach *and* Cheyenne Autumn *in Monument Valley.*

SWAMP ALLIGATOR

Alligators live in the Florida Everglades, a large, low-lying area of swamps, mangroves and forests near Miami. In summer, the swamps dry up, and alligators go in search of new waterholes.

♦

GIANT TREES

Giant sequoias are among the world's biggest and oldest trees. They grow only on the western slopes of the Sierra Nevada mountains in California, in places such as Yosemite National Park (left). The largest sequoia, nicknamed the "General Sherman," is 275 ft. (84 m) high and 102 ft. (31m) around the base. It may be as much as 2,500 years old.

♦ *A sequoia's thick bark protects it from fire and disease. But lightning can seriously damage the tree.*

NATIONAL PARKS

The USA created the world's first national park, Yellowstone, in 1872. There are now over 60 major national parks, covering over 2 percent of the country's area. Some of the main ones are shown below. Some parks help to build up numbers of animals. Others simply protect animals such as wolves from being hunted. Many parks preserve spectacular natural scenery.

Olympic Park, Washington, preserves a stretch of rugged coastline.

Yellowstone Park, Wyoming, is famous for its hot springs and geysers.

Isle Royale, Michigan, is a large island on Lake Superior where you can see beavers.

Shenandoah, Virginia, is in the beautiful Blue Ridge Mountains.

Yosemite National Park in the Sierra Nevada mountains, California, has jagged peaks and beautiful lakes and waterfalls.

Petrified Forest, Arizona, has ancient trees that have turned into rock.

In Mammoth Cave, Kentucky, you can explore huge caverns.

— Bobolink

ON THE GREAT PLAINS

The grasslands of the Great Plains extend right down the U.S.A., from the Canadian border to Texas, and across country from the foothills of the Rockies to the Missouri river. Grasses grow quickly in the short, hot summers, and flowers, such as poppies and mallows fill the fields. Trees are rare. Vast herds of buffalo used to roam these plains, but they were hunted almost to extinction. Now those that are left live mainly in parks and reserves. Prairie dogs live together in colonies called "towns", made up of millions of animals.

♦ *The pronghorn can run at speeds of up to 40 m.p.h. (65 kph) across the Great Plains.*

Gopher

MOUNTAIN LION

Mountain lions, also called cougars, are lone hunters, each with it's own territory ranging up to 19 sq. mi. (50 sq km). The young stay with their mother for a year before venturing off on their own. Mountain lions can leap 20 ft. (6m)

♦ *Mountain lions were once hunted because they were thought to be a danger to cattle.*

DAMS AND LODGES

Beavers are good swimmers and can stay under water for up to 15 minutes. They can gnaw through tree trunks with their sharp teeth, and they build dams with the branches. The dams create ponds that make it easier for beavers to catch fish.

♦ *Beavers build homes, called lodges, with sticks, mud and stones. The lodges have an underwater entrance.*

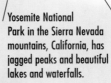

CITY WILDLIFE

When their natural habitats are destroyed by humans, some animals adapt to city life. Raccoons (left) are mischievous animals, hiding out in garages and empty buildings. At night they search for scraps from garbage cans.

♦ *Raccoons are very skilful with their paws and have been known to open refrigerators.*

United States of America:
Farming and industry

The United States has the world's richest economy. It manufactures and sells more products than any other country. Americans have achieved this powerful position by using their natural resources wisely, by making many important scientific discoveries, and by working hard. There are huge farmlands across the country, where farmers grow wheat, corn, and many kinds of fruit and vegetables. The raising of cattle, sheep and chickens is also an important business. In the past, coal and iron ore helped build the country's mighty manufacturing industries. These resources are now running out, but in recent years, oil has been found in Alaska and the states around the Gulf of Mexico. New electronics and aircraft industries have sprung up in Texas, California and Washington. In the big cities, there are bankers, publishers, film-makers and musicians, all spreading American influence to the rest of the world.

FIELDS OF CALIFORNIA

Many crops, such as these pumpkins, need good soil, plenty of sun, and lots of water. California has the soil and sun, but water has to be brought in from wetter areas. Dams, aqueducts, and canals transport water from the Sierra Nevada mountains and the Colorado River to the farmlands.

KENNEDY SPACE CENTER

A space shuttle blasts off from Kennedy Space Center (below), at Cape Canaveral in Florida. The shuttle can carry up to seven astronauts and scientists into orbit and back. After two minutes, the shuttle's two solid-fuel rocket boosters drop away and fall to Earth by parachute. Six minutes later, its external fuel tank is jettisoned to disintegrate in the atmosphere. When its mission is finished, the shuttle slows down from 17,400 m.p.h. (28,000 kph) in space to land back on Earth at 208 m.p.h. (335 kph).

♦ *In 1969, the American astronaut Neil Armstrong was the first on the moon.*

DISNEY

Walt Disney made his first Mickey Mouse cartoon in 1928. Today, his company is one of the biggest in the world's entertainment industry, making films such as *The Lion King* and *Hercules*. The company has theme parks in California and Florida (right), as well as in Tokyo and Paris.

♦ *Disney's first long cartoon was Snow White and the Seven Dwarfs, released in 1937.*

LAKESIDE CITY

Chicago, Illinois (right), is the third largest city in the U.S.A. It lies at the southern end of Lake Michigan. The city was founded in 1803 and has changed with the times. It started as a center for processing and distributing agricultural goods, such as grain, timber and meat. Later, it had steel mills and chemical plants. Today, it is a financial, printing and educational center.

♦ *The world's first skyscrapers were built in Chicago in the 1880s. Today, its tallest building is the Sears Tower, which soars to 1,453 ft. (443 m).*

CATTLE DRIVE

In the 1800s, cowboys herded millions of longhorn cattle along the Chisholm Trail from San Antonio, Texas, to Abilene, Kansas. Today, the main cattle-ranching region is in the drier parts of the Great Plains, from Texas to North Dakota. The cattle are rounded up in the fall (left), taken to feeders for fattening, and then shipped to stockyards for slaughter.

♦ *Cowboys are still used to herd cattle.*

TRUCKING

Three-quarters of industrial goods in the U.S. are moved by trucks. These trucks, called rigs or semis, have a tractor unit with a driver's cab, and a separate semi-trailer for the cargo. The cab often has a bed, a microwave oven, and a TV. Truck drivers may travel 93,000 mi. (150,000 km) a year.

♦ *U.S. interstate highways are numbered. Odd numbers run north–south, such as I-5 from Seattle to San Diego. Even numbers run east–west, such as I-10 from Jacksonville to Los Angeles.*

THE AUTOMOBILE

The mass production of automobiles started in 1913 in Detroit, Michigan. Henry Ford's workers made the first automobile that many people could afford, called the Model T. It was nicknamed the "Tin Lizzie", and by the early 1920s, half the automobiles in the world were Model T Fords! Detroit is still the center of the U.S. auto industry, making a quarter of all the automobiles driven by Americans. Today, the manufacturing process (right) is more automated.

♦ *Americans own 194 million automobiles, over a third of the world's total. The three top U.S. car-makers, General Motors, Ford, and Chrysler are among the biggest companies in the world.*

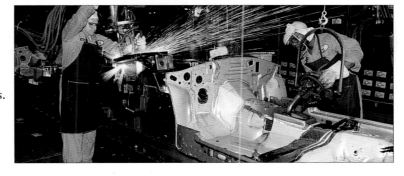

ANTIGUA AND BARBUDA
Area: 171 sq. mi.
Population: 68,720

BAHAMAS
Area: 5,382 sq. mi.
Population: 301,800

BARBADOS
Area: 166 sq. mi.
Population: 279,500

BELIZE
Area: 8,867 sq. mi.
Population: 279,500

COSTA RICA
Area: 19,730 sq. mi.
Population: 4,016,200

CUBA
Area: 42,804 sq. mi.
Population: 11,346,700

DOMINICA
Area: 290 sq. mi.
Population: 69,030

DOMINICAN REPUBLIC
Area: 18,704 sq. mi.
Population: 8,950,000

EL SALVADOR
Area: 8,124 sq. mi.
Population: 6,704,900

Mexico, Central America
and the Caribbean
People and places

Mexico is a long, narrow country with the Pacific Ocean to the west and the Gulf of Mexico to the east. To the south are seven smaller countries that form a strip of land known as Central America. Across the Caribbean Sea, stretching in a crescent from South America toward Florida and Mexico, are the Caribbean islands, or the West Indies. Mexico and the countries of Central America were the home to great civilizations, such as the Aztecs and the Mayans. After the 1500s, people from all over the world came to Mexico, Central America, and the Caribbean.

OLMEC SCULPTURE

The Olmecs were one of the oldest civilizations in Mexico. They lived from about 1200 to 400 B.C. The Olmecs carved giant stone heads, some 10 ft. (3 m) high. These stones may have shown the faces of people sacrificed to Olmec gods.
♦ *The Olmecs and the Aztecs worshipped the snake and the jaguar.*

The border between Mexico and the U.S.A. runs along the Rio Grande river For almost 1,240 mi. (2,000 km). Mexicans call the river the **Rio Bravo**.

Modern Mexico City was built on top of the ruins of the Aztec capital of Tenochtitlán.

Map labels: Tijuana, Mexicali, U.S.A., Ciudad Juárez, Hermosillo, Chihuahua, Baja California, Gulf of California, Rio Bravo/Grande, SIERRA MADRE OCCIDENTAL, SIERRA MADRE ORIENTAL, MEXICO, Culiacán, Monterrey, Matamoros, Durango, GULF OF MEXICO, Tropic of Cancer, Aguascalientes, Tampico, León, Bay of Campeche, Campeche, Méri, Yucatan Peninsula, Guadalajara, Manzanillo, Mexico City, Puebla, Veracruz, Citlaltépetl, Belize, Belmopan, Balsas, Coatzacoalcos, Acapulco, Oaxaca, Gulf of Tehuantepec, GUATEMALA, PACIFIC OCEAN, Guatemala City, San Salvador, EL SALVADOR

PIÑATA PARTY

A favorite children's party game in Mexico is breaking the piñata. The piñata is a clay pot or papier-mâché animal suspended by a rope, and filled with candy, fruit, and toys. Children, wearing a blindfold, take turns to try and break the piñata with a stick. The treats fall to the ground for all the children to share.
♦ *Every Mexican town and village has its own special fiesta, or holiday, to honour its patron saint.*

MAYAN CITY

Tikal, in Guatemala, was once a great Mayan city with 45,000 inhabitants. Between 200 B.C. and A.D. 900, the Mayans built stone palaces and pyramids topped by temples (below). The Mayans recorded time with calendars and made accurate measurements of the movement of the sun and moon.
♦ *The Mayans could predict eclipses.*

MEXICAN WEAVING

The Mexican state of Oaxaca is home to Zapotecs, Mixtecs, and other Native Americans who create their own traditional crafts. Zapotec women are famous for weaving colorful, detailed designs (left).
♦ *Some villages have specialized in the same designs for centuries.*

GRENADA — Area: 133 sq. mi. Population: 89,500

GUATEMALA — Area: 42,042 sq. mi. Population: 14,655,200

HAITI — Area: 10,569 sq. mi. Population: 8,121,600

HONDURAS — Area: 43,277 sq. mi. Population: 6,975,200

JAMAICA — Area: 4,244 sq. mi. Population: 2,731,800

MEXICO — Area: 756,066 sq. mi. Population: 106,202,900

NICARAGUA — Area: 46,467 sq. mi. Population: 5,465,100

PANAMA — Area: 29,762 sq. mi. Population: 3,039,200

ST. KITTS AND NEVIS — Area: 104 sq. mi. Population: 38,960

CARIBBEAN VILLAGE

This village on the island of St. Lucia, is typical of the Caribbean. The forest has been cleared for small farms, where people grow vegetables, such as cassava, yams, and sweet potatoes, and fruits, such as plantains and bananas. Farmers sell their produce at markets.

♦ *Many of St. Lucia's people are descended from African slaves.*

When Christopher Columbus sailed to the **Caribbean islands** in 1492, he thought he was in the East Indies and called the people who live there "Indians".

DAY OF THE DEAD

In Mexico, the Day of the Dead is celebrated on November 2 . People visit the graves of their relatives, lighting candles and bringing food to the cemetery. Shops sell candy and chocolates shaped like skulls (above).

♦ *On December 12th, Mexicans honor Our Lady of Guadalupe, the country's patron saint.*

Map

BAHAMAS

Nassau
Andros I.
Tropic of Cancer

ATLANTIC OCEAN

TURKS & CAICOS ISLANDS (U.K.)

ANGUILLA (U.K.)

VIRGIN Is. (U.S. & U.K.)

Great Inagua

Havana
CUBA
Camagüey
Isla de la Juventud
Yucatan Channel

DOMINICAN REPUBLIC
HAITI
Port-au-Prince
Santo Domingo

San Juan
PUERTO RICO (U.S.A.)

ST KITTS & NEVIS
MONTSERRAT (U.K.)

ANTIGUA & BARBUDA
GUADELOUPE (FR.)
DOMINICA
MARTINIQUE (FR.)
ST. LUCIA
BARBADOS
ST. VINCENT & THE GRENADINES
GRENADA

TRINIDAD & TOBAGO

CAYMAN ISLANDS (U.K.)
Kingston
JAMAICA

GREATER ANTILLES

LESSER ANTILLES

BELIZE

CARIBBEAN SEA

HONDURAS
Tegucigalpa
NICARAGUA
Managua
Lake Nicaragua

ARUBA (NETH.)
NETHERLANDS ANTILLES (NETH.)

San José
COSTA RICA
Panama City
PANAMA
Panama Canal

COLOMBIA

N

Kilometers
0   200   400   600   800   1000

0   200   400   600
Miles

PANAMA CANAL

The opening of the Panama Canal in 1914 allowed ships to pass directly between the Atlantic and Pacific Oceans and saved them the long journey around South America. The Canal is 50 mi. (81 km) long but is too narrow for many modern ships. A wider canal may be built in the future.

♦ *Over 20,000 workers died from tropical diseases while digging the Panama Canal.*

Data file

Area	1,044,664 sq. mi./2,705,661 sq km
Population	185 million
Independent countries	21, and 11 dependencies
Largest country	Mexico (756,067 sq. mi./1,958,201 sq km)
Smallest country	St. Kitts and Nevis (104 sq. mi./269 sq km)
Most populated country	Mexico (106,202,900)
Least populated country	St. Kitts and Nevis (38,960)
Largest cities	Mexico City, Mexico (18.1 million); Havana, Cuba (2.1 million)
Highest mountain	Citlaltépetl, Mexico (18,700 ft./5,699 m)
Longest river	Rio Bravo/Grande (1,886 mi./3,035 km), shared with U.S.A.
Largest lake	Nicaragua, Nicaragua (3,100 sq. mi./8,029 sq km)
Religions	Roman Catholic, Protestant, Hindu
Languages	Spanish, English, French, many Native American languages

How places got their names

Caribbean Sea	after the Carib people
Honduras	from the Spanish *hondas*, meaning depths
Jamaica	from the Arawak for *island of springs*
Martinique	sighted by Columbus on St. Martin's Day, June 15th, 1502
Mexico	from the Aztec name for a lake, meaning *lake of the moon*

ST. LUCIA
Area: 238 sq. mi.
Population: 166,300

ST. VINCENT AND THE GRENADINES
Area: 150 sq. mi.
Population: 117,500

TRINIDAD AND TOBAGO
Area: 1,980 sq. mi.
Population: 1,088,600

Mexico, Central America and the Caribbean:
Nature, farming and industry

This is a region filled with great contrasts, from the dry deserts of northern Mexico to the wet tropical rain forests of Panama. Many kinds of cactus grow in the desert, and there are hummingbirds and orchids in the forest. The volcanic, mountainous islands of the Caribbean are surrounded by warm seas, where turtles and sailfish swim. The islands' rich soils are good for growing crops, such as sugar, coffee, and bananas. Tourists come here for the hot sun, sandy beaches and clear blue waters. The Mexican economy, which is the region's richest, has developed thanks to farming, manufacturing and newly discovered oilfields.

VOLCANIC ISLANDS

The larger Caribbean islands are the peaks of an ocean mountain chain. The smaller islands of the Lesser Antilles are volcanic. Although many of these volcanoes are extinct, like the Pitons in St Lucia (above right), some are still active. In 1997 the eruption of Mount Soufriere, on Montserrat, forced many people to leave the island.
♦ **The western coast of Central America has many volcanoes and earthquakes. An earthquake destroyed large sections of Mexico City in 1985.**

SAILFISH

Sailfish live in the tropical waters of the Caribbean Sea. They are powerful swimmers and are the fastest of all fish. They can reach a speed of 62 m.p.h. (100 kph).
♦ **The fin on a fish's back is called the dorsal fin. Sailfish have an especially big dorsal fin, and a long, swordlike beak.**

Eagle

Saguaro cactus

Roadrunner

Jackrabbit

IN THE DESERT

The Sonoran Desert stretches across northern Mexico and into the U.S.A. Despite the high temperatures and low rainfall, many plants and animals live in these extreme conditions. The saguaro cactus, for example, stores water in its thick trunk. Jack rabbits have big ears that let heat escape from their body. Snakes and mice escape the heat by hiding in burrows by day and only come out to feed at night.
♦ **Although the roadrunner can fly, it prefers to scurry very fast over the ground.**

HURRICANE!

Hurricanes are fierce tropical storms. They often start out in the Atlantic Ocean, before moving across the Caribbean Sea and the Gulf of Mexico. Hurricane winds begin at 75 m.p.h. (120 kph), causing great damage on land to crops and buildings, as well as loss of life.
♦ **The center of a hurricane, where wind speeds are lowest, is called the "eye".**

Path of hurricane

Gila monster

TRADITIONAL FOODS

Mexican farmers grow about 50 kinds of beans, which are used in many traditional dishes. Corn, sometimes known as maize, and squash are also common throughout this region.

♦ *Corn flour is used for making tortillas, a flat Mexican bread.*

Beans   Maize   Squash

MEXICAN OIL

Mexico is one of the world's top oil producers. Oil is found along the Gulf coast and is also drilled offshore. The crude oil is processed at refineries, such as this one at Tula (left). Oil is a major source of income for Mexico.

♦ *Trinidad and Tobago also has oil reserves, and its refineries process oil from Venezuela.*

FOREST LIFE

Forests cover much of southern Central America. Some of the rain forests are hot and steamy all year. Others, such as the cloud forests of Costa Rica, which grow at elevations of 2,950 to 4,900 ft. (900 to 1,500 m) above sea level, are damp and cool, and the trees are covered in lichens and moss. Many years ago, North and South America were separated by ocean. When falling sea levels created a land bridge, animals and plants crossed to Central America. Today, there may be hundreds of types of birds and thousands of different insect species in a small area of forest.

♦ *Bats thrive in Central America's forests. Panama alone has 31 different species. Some eat fruit, others drink nectar, and a few, such as the vampire bat, are carnivores, or meat eaters.*

Howler monkey

Squirrel monkey

Quetzal

Fruit bat

Ocelot

Hummingbird

Poison-arrow frog

MAKING SISAL

The agave plant is common in the Yucatan peninsula of Mexico. Its leaves are cut, and the fibers inside are taken out and dried (above) to make sisal.

♦ *Sisal is used to make ropes.*

CARIBBEAN TOURISM

Because of their ideal climate and warm waters, the Caribbean islands are a favourit tourist destination. Tourists enjoy beach resorts, such as this one on Saintt Thomas (above), one of the U.S. Virgin Islands.

♦ *The smaller Virgin Islands are uninhabited.*

ARGENTINA	BOLIVIA	BRAZIL	CHILE	COLOMBIA	ECUADOR	GUYANA	PARAGUAY	PERU
Area: 1,073,399 sq. mi. Population: 39,537,900	Area: 424,164 sq. mi. Population: 8,857,900	Area: 3,265,076 sq. mi. Population: 186,112,800	Area: 292,135 sq. mi. Population: 15,980,900	Area: 440,831 sq. mi. Population: 42,954,300	Area: 103,930 sq. mi. Population: 13,363,600	Area: 83,044 sq. mi. Population: 765,300	Area: 157,048 sq. mi. Population: 6,347,900	Area: 496,225 sq. mi. Population: 27,925,600

South America
People and places

Modern South America is built on the ruins of ancient civilizations, and is a mixture of traditional Native American villages and huge, modern cities. Brazil and Argentina have some of the biggest cities in the world. The people of South America are a mixture of the descendants of Spanish and Portuguese colonists and native peoples such as the Quechua, who are descendants of the Incas. Half the population of South America lives in Brazil, which covers nearly half the continent.

METALWORKING

Metalwork dating from 1500 B.C. has been found in the Andes mountains. This pendant was made about A.D. 1000.

♦ *Gold was panned from mountain rivers.*

The delta of the **Amazon River** is over 186 mi. (300 km) across and extends 250 mi. (400 km) inland.

Lake Titicaca is the highest navigable lake in the world at an altitude of 12,503 ft. (3,811 m).

BUENOS AIRES

The capital of Argentina (left) is also the country's main port and industrial center. With large communities of people of Italian, Spanish, German, and British ancestry, some districts resemble a European city.

♦ *Natives of Buenos Aires are called porteños, which means "people of the port".*

PEOPLE OF THE ANDES

Many of the Native Americans who live in the Andes mountains are farmers. They grow grain and potatoes, and herd sheep and llamas (below, in a village in Bolivia). Many mountain villages have no electricity.

♦ *The Quechua and the Aymará Native American people make up half of Bolivia's population.*

Cape Horn, where the Pacific Ocean meets the Atlantic, is known to sailors for its violent storms.

The **Falklands** are a colony of the United Kingdom. They are called Islas Malvinas by the Argentinians.

Map labels

CARIBBEAN SEA
Barranquilla
Gulf of Venezuela
Maracaibo
Lake Maracaibo
Caracas
Orinoco
VENEZUELA
Georgetown
Paramaribo
GUYANA
SURINAME
FRENCH GUIANA (FRANCE)
Cayenne
GUIANA HIGHLANDS
Medellín
Bogotá
Cali
Huila
COLOMBIA
Orinoco
Branco
Macapá
Equator
Quito
Chimborazo
Guayaquil
ECUADOR
Putumayo
Japurá
Negro
Amazon
Manaus
Belém
São Lu
Marañón
Juruá
Purus
Madeira
Tapajós
Xingu
SELVAS
Tocantins
Nevado Huascarán
PERU
Serra dos Parecis
Guaporé
Arinos
Araguaia
Paranaíba
BRAZIL
Lima
PLANALTO DO MATO GROSSO
Lake Titicaca
Nevado Ancohume
La Paz
BOLIVIA
Mamoré
Brasília
Arica
Lake Poopó
ALTIPLANO
ATACAMA DESERT
ANDES
Belo Horizo
Represa Ilha Grande
Rio de Janei
Tropic of Capricorn
Antofagasta
Volcán Llullaillaco
CHILE
Nevado Ojos del Salado
GRAN CHACO
Pilcomayo
PARAGUAY
Asunción
Iguaçu Falls
São Paulo
SERRA DO MAR
PACIFIC OCEAN
Salado
Uruguay
Pôrto Alegre
Córdoba
ARGENTINA
URUGUAY
Cerro Aconcagua
Rosario
Montevideo
Buenos Aires
River Plate
Santiago
Salado
PAMPAS
Bahía Blanca
Colorado
Negro
Chubut
FALKLAND ISLANDS (U.K.)
Punta Arenas
Strait of Magellan
Tierra del Fuego
Cape Horn

N

Kilometers
0 200 400 600 800 1000

0 200 400 600
Miles

SURINAME
Area: 63,251 sq. mi.
Population: 438,100

URUGUAY
Area: 67,574 sq. mi.
Population: 3,415,900

VENEZUELA
Area: 352,144 sq. mi.
Population: 25,375,300

INCA RUINS

All that is left of Machu Picchu (left) in Peru is ruins, but once it was a holy city of the mighty Inca empire. The Incas ruled over the people of the Andes from Colombia to northern Chile. They built suspension bridges, which were unknown in Europe. They cut stone blocks with such precision that their buildings and palaces needed no mortar. Their empire was destroyed by Spanish invaders in 1532.

♦ **Machu Picchu was mysteriously abandoned by the Incas and rediscovered in 1911.**

FOREST PEOPLE

The Yanomami are the largest forest tribe, and they are among the last to give up their traditional ways of life. They live in villages in the Amazon rain forest (below), on the border of Brazil and Venezuela. Their numbers were once much greater but only about 19,000 are left. Many died from diseases brought by to South America by Europeans.

♦ **In 1998, fires swept through many parts of the Amazon rain forest, destroying large areas of Yanomami lands.**

TLANTIC OCEAN

● Fortaleza

● Recife

São Francisco

● Maceió

gem de dinho

lvador ●

Tropic of Capricorn

Where the **Amazon River** enters the sea, fresh water flows 155 mi. (250 km) out into the Atlantic Ocean.

In 1960, **Brasília** replaced Rio de Janeiro as the capital of Brazil.

RIO CARNIVAL

The annual carnival in Rio de Janeiro, Brazil, is a festival of colorful parades, fancy-dress parties, and samba. This exciting form of music and dance was invented in Brazil, blending African and European rhythms.

♦ **Carnival is based on a Christian tradition of feasting before the period of fasting called Lent.**

SOCCER CRAZY

One thing that unites South America is a passion for soccer. The continent has some of the biggest stadiums and most fanatical soccer fans in the world. South American teams and players such as Pelé, Maradona, and Ronaldo, rank among the best to have played the game. Soccer was introduced by British railway engineers in the early 1900s. Uruguay was the first country to host soccer's top competition, the World Cup, in 1930.

♦ **Since 1930, Brazil has proved to be the most successful World Cup soccer nation.**

Data file

Area	6,858,673 sq. mi./17,763,843 sq km
Population	382 million
Independent countries	12, and 2 dependencies
Largest country	Brazil (3,265,076 sq. mi./8,456,508 sq km)
Smallest country	Suriname (63,251 sq. mi./163,820 sq km)
Most populated country	Brazil (186,112,800)
Least populated country	Suriname (438,100)
Largest cities	Buenos Aires, Argentina (13 million); São Paulo, Brazil (17.7 million); Bogotá, Columbia (7.7 million)
Highest mountain	Aconcagua, Argentina (22,834 ft./6,960 m)
Longest river	Amazon (3,969 mi./6,387 km)
Largest lake	Maracaibo, Venezuela (5,120 sq. mi./13,261 sq km)
Religions	Roman Catholic, Protestant
Languages	Spanish, Portuguese, Native American languages

How places got their names

Amazon	from a Native American word for *big wave*
Bogotá	after a Native American chief
Brazil	from the Portuguese for *red wood dye*
Buenos Aires	from the Spanish for *good winds*, short for Nuestra Señora Santa Maria del Buen Aire, the patron saint of sailors
Tierra del Fuego	from the Spanish for *land of fires*, after the Portuguese explorer Ferdinand Magellan saw bonfires on the shore
Venezuela	from Spanish, meaning *little Venice*

South America: *Nature*

South America has two great natural features that shape the landscape: the Andes mountains and the Amazon River. The Andes extend all the way down the western edge of the continent, from warm, tropical Colombia to the cold lands of southern Chile and Argentina. The Amazon, the world's second longest river, begins high in the mountains of Peru, not far from the Pacific Ocean, and flows through a huge tropical rain forest all the way to the Atlantic. South America also has grasslands, swamps, and cold deserts. These amazing landscapes are home to a greater variety of wildlife than any other continent.

IN THE ANDES MOUNTAINS

The mountains of the Andes rise steeply from the Pacific coast. The slopes have many different habitats because of the rapid changes in altitude. There are farmlands in the foothills, which give way to high, empty plains. Higher up there are glaciers and snow-covered peaks, even close to the Equator. This view over the Chilean Andes (above) was taken from the Orsono volcano.

♦ *The Andes, the world's longest mountain range, are 4,470 mi. (7,200 km) long.*

ATACAMA DESERT

Wind-sculpted rock formations and salt deposits are found in the Valley of the Moon (left), in the Atacama Desert. This part of northern Chile is rich in minerals. The cool, barren lands of the Atacama are one of the driest places on Earth. In some areas of the desert, rain has never been known to fall.

♦ *Plants grow even in the Atacama Desert. They absorb moisture from coastal fogs.*

IGUAÇU FALLS

The spectacular Iguaçu Falls, in southern Brazil, are made up of 275 cascades. Water plunges over the Paraná Plateau, across a gulf 2.5 mi. (4 km) wide. The name, Iguaçu, means "great waters" in the language of the local Guaraní people.

♦ *Near the falls is one of the world's biggest dams, Itaipú, built jointly by Brazil and Paraguay.*

Marine iguana

Frigate bird

San Salvador

Fernandina

Santa Cruz

Isabela

THE GALÁPAGOS ISLANDS

These unique islands lie about 620 mi. (1,000 km) off the coast of Ecuador. When the naturalist, Charles Darwin, visited the islands in 1835, he saw species of animals that were slightly different from those on the mainland. From his observations, Darwin developed a theory of evolution. The theory stated that tiny changes in a species of plant or animal over long periods of time lead to major variations and even new species.

♦ *The islands take their name from the galápago, or giant tortoise.*

San Cristóbal

Santa Maria

Espanola

Giant tortoise

Galápagos Islands

THE SHRINKING FOREST

The Amazon rain forest covers about 2.3 million sq. mi. (6 million sq km) across parts of nine countries. It is being cleared of trees at an alarming rate. Cattle ranches, farms, dams, and mines destroy the forest. Deforestation causes many problems. It leads to flooding, soil erosion, and the extinction of animals and plants. It forces native peoples to change their way of life. Massive burning of trees adds to the greenhouse gases that cause global warming.

One fifth of the world's bird species are found in the Amazon rain forest.

Dams built at Tucuruí and Balbina flooded large areas of land and drowned the forests.

Brazil is the world's second largest producer of tropical timber, after India.

In 4 sq. mi. (10 sq km) of rain forest, there may be up to 1,500 different species of flowers, 400 species of birds, and 150 species of butterflies.

As many as 90 Amazonian tribes disappeared in the 1900s, as parts of their rain forest home were cleared.

Between 1960 and 1990 almost a fifth of South America's tropical rainforest cover was cleared.

Tropical forest
Deforested areas

LIFE IN THE TROPICAL RAIN FOREST

Tropical forests such as the Amazon rain forest, are warm and wet all year round. A tenth of the world's species of animals and plants live in the rain forest. The trees are so dense that little light reaches the forest floor. Toucans and macaws fly through the air, and monkeys swing through the trees using their tails as a fifth limb. On the ground, jaguars hunt at night, and a species of forest spider with a leg-span of up to 8 in. (20 cm) searches for small mammals and birds.

♦ *The jaguar is an excellent swimmer and often catches fish.*

MAGELLAN PENGUINS

Magellan penguins live at the southern tip of South America and on the Falkland Islands. They lay their eggs in burrows or under rocks. Because the summer is so short and the winter so cold, the chicks have to grow up fast.

♦ *Magellan penguins are closely related to the Galápagos species, the most northerly of all penguins.*

Macaw

Sloth

Tamarin

Vampire bat

Bird-eating spider

Toucan

Jaguar

South America:
Farming and industry

South America is often thought of as being part of the developing world, but it does not lack resources and industries. It has modern, thriving cities, though many city-dwellers live in slum housing. Brazil's economy is bigger than that of Russia. It is a major steel and automobile producer . South American countries grow and export many foods and farm products. Coffee, cocoa, sugar, and soybeans are grown on large plantations. Brazil produces more fruit than any other country, including oranges, pineapples, and bananas. Small farmers grow cassava in warm areas and potatoes in the mountains. Mountain people also herd llamas and alpacas for their meat and wool. Forest-dwellers tap rubber trees and gather nuts, fruit, and honey for sale at markets. South America also has many deposits of minerals and fossil fuels.

GAUCHOS

Gauchos are Argentina's cowboys, famous for their horsemanship. They herd cattle on the country's vast pampas, or grassy plains. Gauchos wear black hats and riding trousers called bombachas.

♦ *Argentina and Brazil are both major beef-producing countries.*

GROWING COFFEE

Coffee comes from a shrub, or small tree, that grows best in highland regions in the tropics (below). The shrubs produce berries that look like bright red cherries. The berries are picked by hand, or by a machine that shakes them off the trees, and the outer pulp is removed. Inside each coffee berry are two beans. These beans are dried in the sun before their skin is removed and they are roasted in big ovens.

♦ *Brazil and Colombia are the world's two leading producers of coffee. The coffee plant originally grew in East Africa.*

TOY MAKING

The native peoples of South America made toys out of the things they found around them. They made dolls from dried corn husks and sticks. Around Lake Titicaca, in Peru, children were given tiny models of the reed boats that sailed on the lake. In Colombia, people made ceramic birds, while Brazilians crafted pottery whistles shaped like animals. The toy-making tradition is kept alive today, but with more modern toys, such as buses (right), automobiles, and airplanes.

♦ *The toys made by people of the Xingu region of Brazil are highly prized by museums and collectors around the world.*

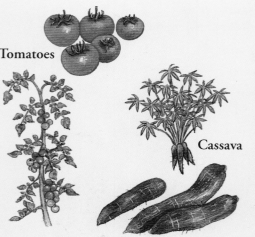

COMMON CROPS

Some foods that are eaten every day around the world originally came from South America. They were taken to Europe by Spanish conquerors in the 1500s. Today, cassava, also called manioc, is an important part of the diet of many Africans. Potatoes are the world's most commonly grown vegetable, and tomatoes are also popular.

♦ *Potatoes are rich in starch, high in protein, and contain important vitamins and minerals.*

Tomatoes

Potatoes

Cassava

BUILDING AIRCRAFT

Brazil is the main manufacturing country in South America and has the world's tenth largest industrial economy. Brazilian industry has grown rapidly since the 1960s. Much of it is based on the use of local raw materials. The government supported industries, such as clothing, textiles, food processing, and shipbuilding. It also helped set up a company to build small aircraft. The roads in many regions of Brazil are not dependable, so people rely on airplanes to get to remote areas. Brazil also makes military airplanes (below) and has become the world's sixth largest manufacturer of aircraft.

♦ *Brazilian industry is centered in the region around São Paulo, which produces 80 percent of the country's industrial goods.*

FISHING

The Pacific waters off the coast of Peru and Chile contain some of the world's richest fishing grounds. The Humboldt current flows from the south bringing cold water that is rich in plankton, the tiny sea creatures on which many fish feed. Peruvian trawlers use nets to catch sardines and anchovies, and individual fishermen catch much bigger fish (below). Chileans catch hake, swordfish, sole and conger eels.

♦ *Peru's fish catch decreases when the cold waters off its coast are occasionally replaced by warmer tropical currents.*

MINING AND MINERALS

The native peoples of South America worked with precious metals, and the Spanish colonists searched for gold, silver, and tin. Many of the old mines are now exhausted, but minerals continue to be very important to the continent's economies. Brazil is the largest producer of iron ore in the world. Copper makes up 40 percent of Chile's exports. Venezuela is a leading oil producer, and new oilfields have been discovered in Colombia and Peru.

Coal is found in the Cauca Valley region of the Colombian Andes.

Mining makes up about a tenth of Peru's total economy.

Tin is the major source of Bolivia's export earnings.

Chile is the world's leading producer of copper.

Venezuela has more oil reserves than any other South American country.

Brazil produces over 148 million tons (150 million tonnes) of iron ore a year; this is almost one sixth of the world's total output.

Coal
Oil
Iron ore
Copper
Silver
Bauxite
Gold
Tin

CHILEAN COPPER

The world's largest open-pit copper mine is in Chuquicamata, Chile (above). The giant hole in the ground measures 3 mi. by 1.6 mi. (4.8 km by 2.5 km), and one half of all Chile's copper comes from this one mine. Dynamite is used to blast out the ore, which is loaded onto giant trucks. Each day, 150 trucks take away 541,000 tons (550,000 tonnes) of ore. They take it to a plant where it is crushed, mixed with water, and then mashed. The copper is smelted at high temperatures into ingots. This process creates dangerous by-products, such as sulphur and arsenic.

♦ *Copper can be shaped quite easily and is a good conductor of heat and electricity. These features make it ideal for use in electrical cables and other electrical components.*

DENMARK Area: 16,638 sq. mi. Population: 5,432,300

ESTONIA Area: 17,400 sq. mi. Population: 1,332,900

FINLAND Area: 130,559 sq. mi. Population: 5,223,400

ICELAND Area: 39,768 sq. mi. Population: 296,700

IRELAND Area: 27,137 sq. mi. Population: 4,015,700

LATVIA Area: 24,900 sq. mi. Population: 2,290,200

LITHUANIA Area: 25,200 sq. mi. Population: 3,596,600

NORWAY Area: 125,050 sq. mi. Population: 4,593,000

SWEDEN Area: 173,732 sq. mi. Population: 9,001,800

Northern *Europe*
People and places

The countries of northern Europe all have distinct identities, but they also have many things in common. The people of Iceland, Norway, Sweden, Denmark, and the Faeroe Islands are descendants of the Vikings, and their languages come from Old Norse, the language of the Vikings. English, the main language of the United Kingdom, which includes England, Scotland, Wales and Northern Ireland, also contains many Norse words, because Vikings settled in the region in the 8th and 9th centuries.

TRADITIONAL WAYS

Along the rugged coasts and on the islands of northern Europe, people farm and fish in traditional ways. This Faeroe islander (right) is shearing a sheep.
♦ **The Faeroes are a group of 22 islands in the north Atlantic. They belong to Denmark.**

Arctic Circle

Reykjavik

ICELAND

Vatnajökullia is a huge icecap on Iceland. It covers eight percent of the country.

FAEROE ISLANDS (DENMARK)

N

Kilometers

0   100   200   300   400   500

0   100   200   300
Miles

A T L A N T I C

O C E A N

Shetland Islands

STONEHENGE

Stonehenge is a mysterious group of standing stones, built between about 3000 and 1500 B.C., in southern England. No one really knows why Stonehenge was built. It might have been used as a center of worship or as a way of predicting eclipses of the sun and moon.
♦ **Some of the giant stones were transported from the distant mountains of Wales.**

Scotland voted to have its own parliament in 1997, but it remains a part of the United Kingdom.

Orkney Islands

Hebrides

SCOTLAND

Glasgow   ● Edinburgh

NORTHERN IRELAND

Belfast

IRELAND   *Isle of Man*

Dublin   *IRISH SEA*

NORTH SEA

PENNINES

Manchester   ● Leeds

● Cork

Cork is the second largest city in the Republic of Ireland, after Dublin. It was originally a Viking fort.

WALES   *Severn*

UNITED KINGDOM

● Birmingham

ENGLAND

Cardiff ●

London

Thames

A barrier across the **Thames River** protects London from flooding. The barrier can be lowered if the water level is too high.

ENGLISH CHANNEL

FRANCE

SENTRY DUTY

In England, there are many colorful ceremonies associated with the royal family. This sentry is a member of one of the seven army regiments that take turns guarding the Queen. Every June, there is a spectacular parade, called the "Trooping of the Color" near Buckingham Palace, in London. The Guards parade in front of the Queen.
♦ **Norway, Sweden, and Denmark also have royal families.**

TOWN AND COUNTRY

England changed from a farming to an industrial nation during the 1700s. In about 1850, it became the first country in which the majority of people lived in cities rather than villages. Rural life, however, is still very important. Widecombe in the Moor in southwest England (right) is a typical English village. Its church tower dates from the 16th century.
♦ **Many of Britain's favorite paintings, poems, and TV series focus on village life.**

VIKING LEGACY

This is the prow of a Viking longship. The Vikings were seafaring people who spread across Scandinavia in the 8th century. They sailed to Iceland and Greenland, and reached North America 500 years before Columbus.

♦ **Longships were built with overlapping planks held together by iron rivets.**

Finland has more than 60,000 lakes. The Finnish name for the country, *Suomi*, means "land of lakes and marshes".

STOCKHOLM

Stockholm, the capital of Sweden, is built on 14 islands where the Baltic Sea meets Lake Mälaren. The islands are connected by 20 bridges. Stockholm began as a Viking settlement and flourished as a trading center in the Middle Ages.

♦ **The majority of people in Sweden belong to the national Lutheran Church.**

STAVE CHURCH

In Norway, Latvia, and Lithuania, 11th-century Christians built churches entirely out of wood. They were made from planks, like a ship, and are called stave churches. Some are still used for worship.

♦ **A magnificent stave church was built at Borgund in Norway.**

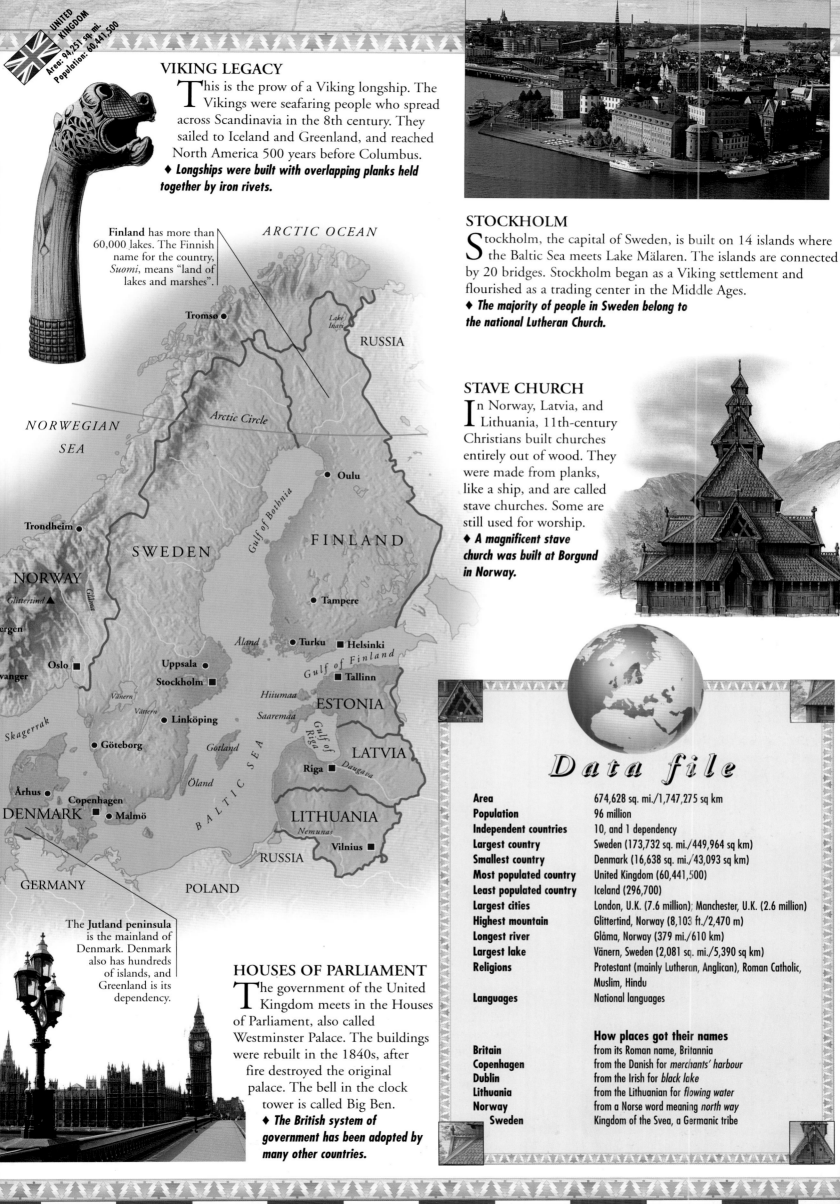

ARCTIC OCEAN

Tromsø

Lake Inari

RUSSIA

NORWEGIAN SEA

Arctic Circle

Trondheim

SWEDEN

Oulu

FINLAND

NORWAY

Glittertind ▲

Bergen

Tampere

Oslo

avanger

Gulf of Bothnia

Glåma

Åland

Turku

Helsinki

Uppsala

Stockholm

Gulf of Finland

Tallinn

Vänern

Hiiumaa

Vättern

Linköping

Saaremaa

ESTONIA

Skagerrak

Göteborg

Gotland

Gulf of Riga

LATVIA

Öland

Riga

Daugava

Århus

Copenhagen

BALTIC SEA

LITHUANIA

DENMARK

Malmö

Nemunas

Vilnius

RUSSIA

GERMANY

POLAND

The **Jutland peninsula** is the mainland of Denmark. Denmark also has hundreds of islands, and Greenland is its dependency.

HOUSES OF PARLIAMENT

The government of the United Kingdom meets in the Houses of Parliament, also called Westminster Palace. The buildings were rebuilt in the 1840s, after fire destroyed the original palace. The bell in the clock tower is called Big Ben.

♦ **The British system of government has been adopted by many other countries.**

Data file

Area	674,628 sq. mi./1,747,275 sq km
Population	96 million
Independent countries	10, and 1 dependency
Largest country	Sweden (173,732 sq. mi./449,964 sq km)
Smallest country	Denmark (16,638 sq. mi./43,093 sq km)
Most populated country	United Kingdom (60,441,500)
Least populated country	Iceland (296,700)
Largest cities	London, U.K. (7.6 million); Manchester, U.K. (2.6 million)
Highest mountain	Glittertind, Norway (8,103 ft./2,470 m)
Longest river	Glåma, Norway (379 mi./610 km)
Largest lake	Vänern, Sweden (2,081 sq. mi./5,390 sq km)
Religions	Protestant (mainly Lutheran, Anglican), Roman Catholic, Muslim, Hindu
Languages	National languages

How places got their names

Britain	from its Roman name, Britannia
Copenhagen	from the Danish for *merchants' harbour*
Dublin	from the Irish for *black lake*
Lithuania	from the Lithuanian for *flowing water*
Norway	from a Norse word meaning *north way*
Sweden	Kingdom of the Svea, a Germanic tribe

31

Northern Europe:
Nature, farming and industry

Northern Europe stretches from northern Norway, which is above the Arctic Circle, to the mild, rainy lowlands of England and Ireland. While Iceland is a cold plateau with active volcanoes, Norway and Sweden are mainly mountainous and forested. Finland and the Baltic countries of Estonia, Latvia and Lithuania are low-lying areas of lakes, rivers, and forests. Most people in northern Europe live and work in cities. Sweden and the United Kingdom are important manufacturing countries, while Norway has become rich from its reserves of oil and natural gas found under the North Sea.

SWEDISH FURNITURE

Half of Sweden is covered by forest, and wood is one of the country's most valuable resources. The trees are mostly coniferous softwoods, such as pine and spruce, and there is also a lot of birch. These trees grow quickly and are easy to cut and shape, which makes them ideal for making furniture. Sweden is one of the world's leading furniture manufacturers.

♦ *Many of Sweden's forests are managed by companies that replant after cutting. The logs are floated down fast-flowing rivers to the sawmills.*

BALTIC SEAL

Seals are mammals that live most of their lives in the sea, although they return to land to breed and sleep. Their limbs are flippers, and they have waterproof fur. Layers of blubber under their skin keep seals warm in icy waters. The Baltic seal (right) lives around the coasts of Finland.

♦ *On land, seals are slow-moving and vulnerable to animal predators and human hunters. In the sea, they are fast, powerful swimmers.*

GIANT'S CAUSEWAY

According to legend, this rocky outcrop on the coast of Northern Ireland is a road built by a giant across the Irish Sea to Scotland. In fact, the causeway was formed by volcanic lava that cooled when it met the sea, forming amazing six-sided pillars of rock.

♦ *Northern Ireland's rich soil was created by rock fragments left behind when the glaciers melted.*

NORTH SEA OIL

Oil was discovered under the North Sea in 1970. Special production platforms were installed, mainly in the waters of Norway, the United Kingdom, and Denmark. Gullfaks C (left) is a huge Norwegian oil and natural gas platform, with a large living space for its workers. Many of the North Sea oilfields are now running low, but new oil has been found in the Atlantic Ocean west of the Shetland Islands.

♦ *The crude oil is refined into fuel for automobiles and airplanes.*

Gannets

DECIDUOUS FORESTS

The warmer parts of northern Europe were once covered in deciduous forest, but much of it has now been cleared for farms and cities. Deciduous trees, such as oak, beech and elm, shed their leaves in winter. Squirrels build nests, called dreys, in the branches of oak trees, and blue tits, woodpeckers, and owls live in the upper canopy. On the forest floor, flowers, such as bluebells and daffodils, come up in spring. Badgers and foxes search for food among the leaves.

♦ *Badgers sleep in their underground homes, called setts, by day. At dusk, they come out to feed on slugs, nuts, berries, and voles.*

Red fox

Hedgehog

Eurasian badger

Oak leaves

Tawny owl

TRAWLING THE SEAS

The seas around northern Europe are rich in fish, such as cod, herring, mackerel and plaice. Iceland's economy depends on fishing, and Denmark is one of the world's biggest exporters of fish. The North Sea and the Atlantic Ocean are often very stormy, and trawling (above) can be dangerous.

♦ *Overfishing and pollution have reduced the North Sea's fish stocks, so in Norway, Scotland, and Sweden fish are farmed in huge nets or tanks.*

Blackbird

Beech leaves

Robin

LIFE ON THE CLIFFS

Cliffs on the coasts of northern Europe are home to huge colonies of seabirds. Some nesting areas contain tens of thousands of birds. Gannets and cormorants build nests out of seaweed, grass, and droppings. Puffins make small burrows on the steep slopes above cliffs. Many birds return to the same spot year after year.

♦ *Gannets are superb divers. They plunge into the sea from a height of up to 100 ft. (nearly 30 m) to seize fish under water.*

Puffins

Cormorant

HERDING REINDEER

In the very northern parts of Norway, the nomadic Sami people herd reindeer as they have done for centuries. The reindeer migrate in huge herds to upland areas to graze in the summer and give birth to calves. As the weather gets cooler, they head for more sheltered, wooded areas. Reindeer feed on lichens, moss, and grasses.

♦ *The region where the Sami live is sometimes called Lapland. The Sami, or Lapps, have their own language and religion.*

ALBANIA	ANDORRA	AUSTRIA	BELGIUM	BOSNIA-HERZEGOVINA	BULGARIA	CROATIA	CZECH REPUBLIC	FRANCE
Area: 11,100 sq. mi. Population: 3,563,100	Area: 181 sq. mi. Population: 70,550	Area: 32,377 sq. mi. Population: 8,184,700	Area: 11,783 sq. mi. Population: 10,364,400	Area: 19,741 sq. mi. Population: 4,025,500	Area: 42,855 sq. mi. Population: 7,450,300	Area: 21,829 sq. mi. Population: 4,495,900	Area: 30,450 sq. mi. Population: 10,241,300	Area: 210,026 sq. mi. Population: 60...

East, West and South
Europe
People and places

The countries of Europe have many different cultures and customs, but they also have a lot in common. Greek and Roman civilizations influenced European ideas of art, philosophy, and law. Christianity is a shared religion. Centuries of trade and industry helped build up great cities, such as Rome and Paris. In this century, two world wars shattered the entire continent, and the rivalry between capitalist and communist systems of government split it in two. Recently, western European countries have joined together to form the European Union to increase peace and prosperity.

PARISIAN CAFÉ

Cafés, or coffee houses, are a familiar sight in many European cities. This one, in the Montmatre district of Paris, France, Coffee was introduced into Europe from the East in the 1600s.
♦ *French culture has enriched the world with its writers, painters, philosophers, film directors, and chefs.*

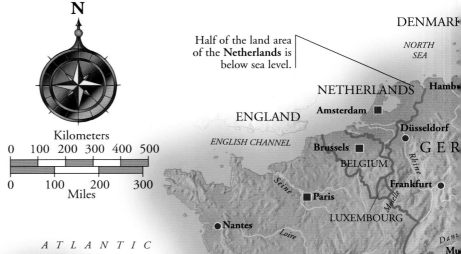

Half of the land area of the **Netherlands** is below sea level.

DELPHI

Ancient Greeks went to the Temple of Apollo at Delphi to consult the oracle, an elderly priestess who made prophecies about the future. Today, the ruined site (left) attracts tourists from around the world.
♦ *The ancient Greeks had many gods. Apollo was the god of music, and poetry and the sun.*

Europe and Africa are separated by the **Strait of Gibraltar**, only 9 mi. (14 km) wide.

BRITTANY

Every year, the Bretons of Brittany, in France, hold a festival called the "Joining of the Hands" (right). It brings together many Celtic people from Scotland, Ireland, Wales, northern Spain, and the Isle of Man.
♦ *The Celtic tribes moved across Europe between 800 B.C. and A.D. 100.*

VENETIAN CARNIVAL

The city of Venice, in Italy, is built in a lagoon on over 100 islands. It has 177 canals, which serve as streets. In early spring, the Venetians hold a carnival. Decorated gondolas are steered by gondoliers in fancy costumes (below).
♦ *Venice is slowly sinking, and many buildings are in peril.*

GERMANY Area: 137,820 sq. mi. Population: 82,431,400
GREECE Area: 50,949 sq. mi. Population: 10,668,300
HUNGARY Area: 35,919 sq. mi. Population: 6,975,200
ITALY Area: 116,324 sq. mi. Population: 58,103,000
LIECHTENSTEIN Area: 62 sq. mi. Population: 33,720
LUXEMBOURG Area: 999 sq. mi. Population: 468,600
MACEDONIA Area: 9,928 sq. mi. Population: 2,045,300
MALTA Area: 122 sq. mi. Population: 398,500
MOLDOVA Area: 13,000 sq. mi. Population: 4,455,500

VILLAGE LIFE

In parts of eastern Europe, life remains traditional. Many people live in small villages and work on farms. This is a typical Romanian village scene.

♦ **More than a third of Romanians are farmers.**

PRAGUE

In Prague, capital of the Czech Republic, there are well-preserved buildings from all periods of history since the Middle Ages. Charlemagne, the first Holy Roman Emporer, was born there in 742. From the 1500s, the city was a center of the Habsburgs, one of Europe's great ruling families. Famous landmarks are the medieval castle on Hradcany hill, the cathedral of St Vitus, and the famous Charles Bridge, built across the Vltava river over 600 years ago.

♦ **An elegant Prague square is named after St. Wencelas (A.D. 907-929), Bohemia's patron saint.**

In the ancient woodland of the **Bialowieza National Park** in Poland, there are bison, wolves, otters, and beavers.

Kyiv, the capital of Ukraine, dates from the 6th century. Vladimir the Great made Christianity the state religion in 988.

Greece has over 2,000 islands, only 170 of which have people living on them.

Map labels

LITHUANIA, RUSSIA, BALTIC SEA, BELARUS, RUSSIA, Leipzig, Warsaw, POLAND, Vistula, Bug, Odra, Desna, Prague, CZECH REPUBLIC, Kyiv, Kharkov, SLOVAKIA, Vienna, Bratislava, UKRAINE, Dnieper, Donetsk, Vistula, MOLDOVA, Dniester, Prut, Kishinev, AUSTRIA, Lake Balaton, Budapest, HUNGARY, CARPATHIANS, SEA OF AZOV, SLOVENIA, Ljubljana, Zagreb, CROATIA, ROMANIA, SAN MARINO, Belgrade, BOSNIA-HERZEGOVINA, Sarajevo, SERBIA AND MONTENEGRO, Bucharest, Danube, BLACK SEA, ADRIATIC SEA, BULGARIA, Sofia, Skopje, MACEDONIA, TURKEY, Tirane, ALBANIA, Naples, GREECE, AEGEAN SEA, IONIAN SEA, Athens, Palermo, MALTA, Crete, Iraklion

NEUSCHWANSTEIN

Europe is full of castles. Many were built for defense, but the fairy-tale-like castle of Neuschwanstein, in southern Germany (left), was built by "mad" King Ludwig II as his place to hide away from the world.

♦ **Almost every room in Ludwig's castle has a swan in its design.**

Data file

Area	1,490,354 sq. mi./3,859,991 sq km
Population	480 million
Independent countries	31
Largest country	Ukraine (233,100 sq. mi./603,700 sq km)
Smallest country	Vatican City (0.17 sq. mi./0.44 sq km)
Most populated country	Germany (82,431,400)
Least populated country	Vatican City (920)
Largest cities	Paris, France (9.6 million); Madrid, Spain (4 million)
Highest mountain	Mont Blanc, France/Italy (15,770 ft./4,807 m)
Longest river	Danube, 6 countries (1,770 mi./2,850 km)
Largest lake	Lake Balaton, Hungary (230 sq. mi./590 sq km)
Religions	Roman Catholic, Protestant, Orthodox, Muslim
Languages	National languages

How places got their names

Alps	from the Celtic word for rock or mountain
Mediterranean	from the Latin for sea in the middle of land
Paris	from a Celtic tribe called the Parisii
Poland	from the Slavonic for low-lying land
Portugal	from the Latin for warm harbor

MONACO Area: 0.75 sq. mi. Population: 32,410
NETHERLANDS Area: 16,163 sq. mi. Population: 16,407,500
POLAND Area: 120,727 sq. mi. Population: 38,635,100
PORTUGAL Area: 35,672 sq. mi. Population: 10,565,200
ROMANIA Area: 91,699 sq. mi. Population: 22,330,000
SAN MARINO Area: 24 sq. mi. Population: 28,880
SLOVAKIA Area: 18,932 sq. mi. Population: 5,431,800
SLOVENIA Area: 7,819 sq. mi. Population: 2,011,700
SPAIN Area: 194,885 sq. mi. Population: 40,341,...

East, West and South Europe:
Nature

Europe is the second smallest continent. It lies between the cold Baltic and North Seas to the north and the warm Mediterranean Sea to the south. For such a small region, there is a remarkable variety of landscapes and habitats. A vast lowland plain, dotted with marshes, lakes, and rivers, stretches from the Netherlands to the Ukraine. Wild animals, such as lynxes and ibexes, live in the mountain ranges of the Alps, Carpathians, and Pyrenees. Because centuries of human habitation have threatened many wild species, Europeans have set aside conservation areas to protect endangered animals and plants.

POSTOGNA CAVES

The limestone rock outcrops of the Balkan Peninsula (between the Adriatic and Aegean Seas) contain many huge cave systems, such as this one in Postogna, Slovenia. Over many years, the river Pivka River has hollowed out over 17 mi. (27 km) of tunnels in the rock. The Concert Hall cave is so big that a symphony orchestra once held a performance inside.
♦ *A blind, colorless salamander lives in these caves. Local people used to think it was a baby dragon.*

Anemone **Fritillary** **Iris** **Cyclamen**

MEDITERRANEAN PLANTS

The Mediterranean has long, hot summers and short, cool winters. Many plants survive the intense heat and drought by flowering only in the spring and fall. In the summer, they die back above ground. They have enough food stored in their bulbs to keep them alive until the next growing season. Anemones, irises, fritillaries, and cyclamens all grow from bulbs.
♦ *Scented herbs, such as lavender, rosemary, sage, and thyme, grow in Mediterranean countries.*

CAMARGUE WETLANDS

The Camargue, in southern France, is one of Europe's most important wetland areas. It covers 300 sq. mi. (800 sq km) at the mouth of the Rhône River where it enters the Mediterranean Sea. The landscape is a mix of fresh and salt water, reed beds, woods, dunes, and lagoons. This varied habitat is home to hundreds of species of plants, birds, and other animals. It is the only European home of the greater flamingo (below). Other birds, such as egrets, bee eaters, hoopoes, and marsh harriers, also live there. Herds of black bulls, used for bullfights, graze in the wetlands.
♦ *An ancient breed of beautiful white horses lives wild in the Camargue wetlands.*

OCELLATED LIZARD

In the warmer regions of Europe, lizards are a familiar sight. They can often be seen basking in the sun on rocks or walls to warm their bodies. The ocellated lizard belongs to a family of green lizards. It grows up to 8 in. (20 cm) long, and is one of the largest European lizards. It likes to live in dry, bushy places.
♦ *Lizards regularly shed their skin. The old dead layer peels off to reveal a new one underneath.*

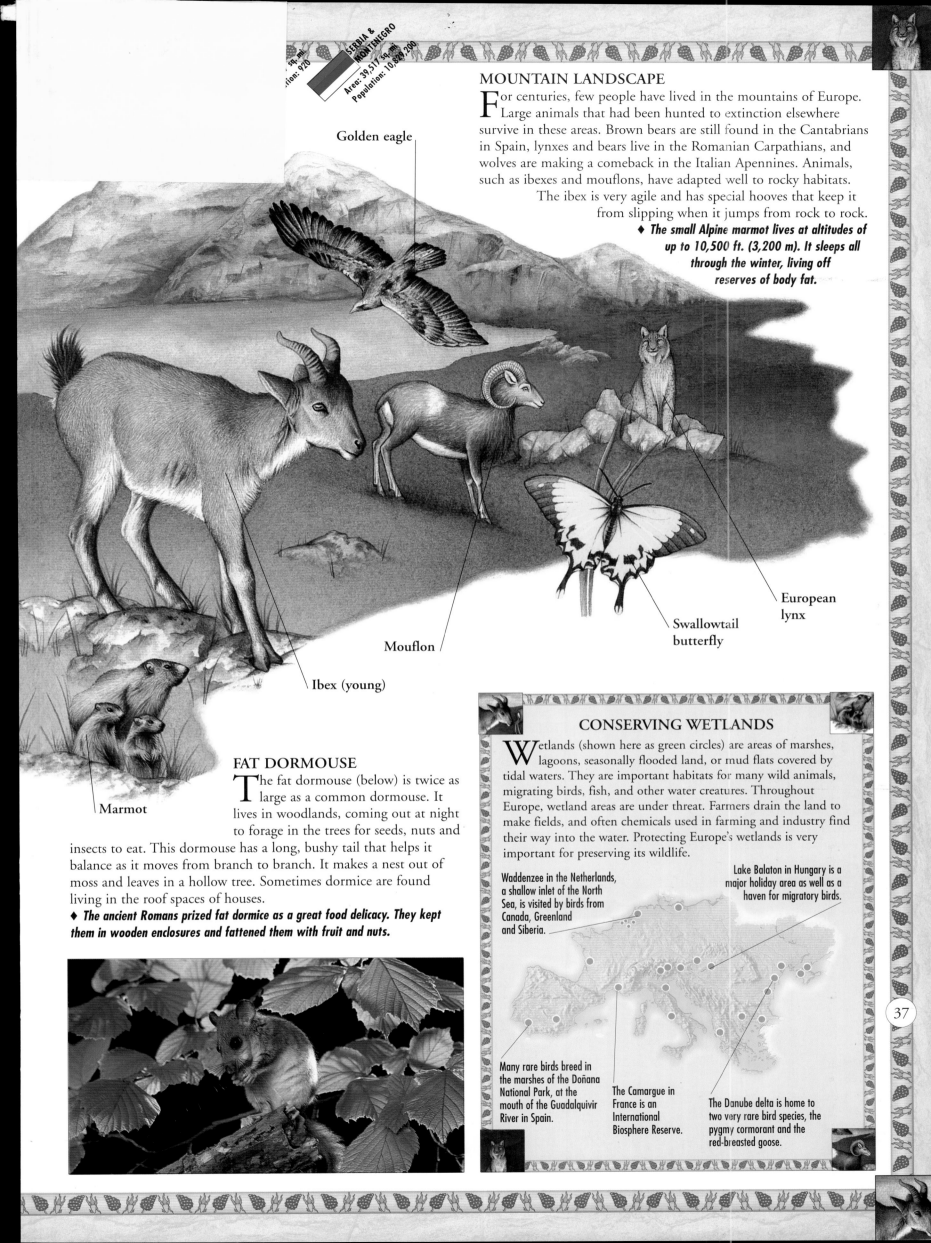

Golden eagle

MOUNTAIN LANDSCAPE

For centuries, few people have lived in the mountains of Europe. Large animals that had been hunted to extinction elsewhere survive in these areas. Brown bears are still found in the Cantabrians in Spain, lynxes and bears live in the Romanian Carpathians, and wolves are making a comeback in the Italian Apennines. Animals, such as ibexes and mouflons, have adapted well to rocky habitats. The ibex is very agile and has special hooves that keep it from slipping when it jumps from rock to rock.

♦ *The small Alpine marmot lives at altitudes of up to 10,500 ft. (3,200 m). It sleeps all through the winter, living off reserves of body fat.*

European lynx

Swallowtail butterfly

Mouflon

Ibex (young)

Marmot

FAT DORMOUSE

The fat dormouse (below) is twice as large as a common dormouse. It lives in woodlands, coming out at night to forage in the trees for seeds, nuts and insects to eat. This dormouse has a long, bushy tail that helps it balance as it moves from branch to branch. It makes a nest out of moss and leaves in a hollow tree. Sometimes dormice are found living in the roof spaces of houses.

♦ *The ancient Romans prized fat dormice as a great food delicacy. They kept them in wooden enclosures and fattened them with fruit and nuts.*

CONSERVING WETLANDS

Wetlands (shown here as green circles) are areas of marshes, lagoons, seasonally flooded land, or mud flats covered by tidal waters. They are important habitats for many wild animals, migrating birds, fish, and other water creatures. Throughout Europe, wetland areas are under threat. Farmers drain the land to make fields, and often chemicals used in farming and industry find their way into the water. Protecting Europe's wetlands is very important for preserving its wildlife.

Waddenzee in the Netherlands, a shallow inlet of the North Sea, is visited by birds from Canada, Greenland and Siberia.

Lake Balaton in Hungary is a major holiday area as well as a haven for migratory birds.

Many rare birds breed in the marshes of the Doñana National Park, at the mouth of the Guadalquivir River in Spain.

The Camargue in France is an International Biosphere Reserve.

The Danube delta is home to two very rare bird species, the pygmy cormorant and the red-breasted goose.

East, West and South Europe:
Farming and industry

For centuries, Europe has been a major center for trade. It is a region rich in natural resources, such as fertile farmland, water, coal, and iron ore. Germany, France, and Italy are among the world's leading industrial nations, while smaller countries, such as Switzerland and Luxembourg, are centers of banking and finance. There are still many rural areas in Europe, especially in the east, where traditional ways of life based on farming continue.

FARMING IN POLAND

In many east European countries, such as Poland and Romania, many farmers cannot afford tractors. They use horses and oxen for plowing, and harvest hay and crops by hand, as these Polish farmers near Zakopane (above) are doing. The hay is fed to farm animals in the winter when there is nothing for them to graze on in the fields.

♦ *Poland's main crops are wheat, barley, rye, and potatoes.*

SUPERCAR

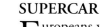

Europeans were among the earliest inventors and makers of gasoline-driven automobiles. Among these car manufacturers were Karl Benz, Armand Peugeot, and Louis Renault, whose names still appear on automobiles. Among the most expensive automobiles are Italian Ferraris (left). The company that makes them was founded by the racing-car driver Enzo Ferrari in 1939.

♦ *Europe's biggest producers of automobiles are Germany, France, Spain, and Italy.*

DUTCH WINDMILL

Before the invention of the steam engine in the 1700s, windmills were used in many parts of Europe for grinding grain into flour. The sails turned grindstones that crushed the grain. In low-lying regions, such as the Netherlands, windmills were also used to pump water from flooded fields (below). Today, more advanced technology is used, but old windmills are a common sight across the landscape.

♦ *Half of the land in the Netherlands is used for farming.*

ROTTERDAM

The port of Rotterdam (above), on the mouth of the Rhine River in the Netherlands, handles more cargo than any other port in the world. Over 40 percent of Europe's ship-carried imports from the United States arrive in Rotterdam, and much of the continent's crude oil is delivered to its oil refineries and chemical works. Many goods arrive in large containers that can be quickly and easily transferred to trucks or smaller cargo boats. These boats can travel to many of Europe's industrial centers along rivers and canals.

♦ *Rotterdam is 19 mi. (30 km) from the North Sea. Ships reach it by the New Waterway, built in 1872.*

SUNFLOWERS

In parts of Europe where the climate is hot and dry, such as the Spanish region of Andalusia (below), sunflowers and fruit such as oranges are grown. Sunflowers are grown commercially for a range of products: the leaves are used to feed animals, and the seeds are crushed to produce oil, which is used for soap and paint or for cooking. The seeds can also be roasted and eaten. Sunflowers also make popular garden plants, growing as high as 16 ft.(5 m).

♦ *Sunflowers come from North America and were brought to Spain in the 1500s. They get their name because their heads turn to follow the sun.*

NUCLEAR POWER

Since France has little coal and gas and no oilfields, the French government decided to use nuclear power to meet the country's energy needs. France's first reactor began operation in 1959. Nuclear power now provides about 75 percent of the country's electricity. These workers at La Hague (above) are building cells for the nuclear reactor. Inside the reactor core, atoms of plutonium or uranium are split, releasing tremendous energy. This process is known as nuclear fission. The energy heats up water into steam, which is used to turn turbines and generate electricity.

♦ *Nuclear power stations need a lot of water to cool the reactor and make steam, so most stations are built on coasts or beside rivers.*

RHINE BARGE

The Rhine River begins in the mountains of the Swiss Alps and flows to the North Sea, passing through Germany and the Netherlands. Canals and other rivers join the Rhine, including a canal which links it to the Danube River. Barges can travel along this route from the North Sea to the Black Sea. Many of these waterways were important in Europe's early industrial revolution, and still are today. Special boats, called pusher barges (left), are used to transport big loads. They can move heavier cargoes than vessels that pull their loads.

♦ *The main cargoes transported along the Rhine are iron ore, coal, oil products, automobiles, and building stone.*

Russia
and its neighbors
People and places

Russia is the world's largest country. It is so big that you cross 11 time zones when you travel its whole width. While people are having breakfast in the west, in the east they are having their evening meal. This vast region, which includes the mainly Muslim countries of central Asia and the small countries around the Caucasus Mountains, was once ruled by the Russian empire and then, from 1922 to 1991, by the Communist Union of Soviet Socialist Republics (U.S.S.R.). Since 1991, many of these formerly Soviet areas have become independent countries.

ST BASIL'S CATHEDRAL

The Cathedral of St. Basil the Blessed stands next to Red Square in Moscow. It was built by the Russian czar, or king, Ivan the Terrible, in the 16th century.

♦ **The cathedral was badly damaged by Napoleon's army in 1812.**

RUSSIAN PRIESTS

These priests (above) belong to the Russian Orthodox Church. Russian Orthodoxy was suppressed by the communist government of the U.S.S.R. After the government collapsed in 1991, people were allowed to go to church again, and the main cathedral in Moscow, the capital of Russia, was rebuilt.

♦ **The Russian Orthodox Church has its own calendar. It celebrates Christmas 13 days after many other Christian churches.**

SOVIET SOUVENIRS

This man is selling old Soviet army hats in a busy shopping district of Moscow. After the fall of Communism many young Russian soldiers found themselves without a job. Selling army goods is one way to make a living.

♦ **In Moscow, it is common to see people selling wild mushrooms they have collected in the woods outside the city.**

In summer, timber is exported from the port of **Arkhangel'sk,** but in winter, the port is frozen.

In 1961, the first spaceship with a person on board took off from from **Baikonur,** Kazakhstan.

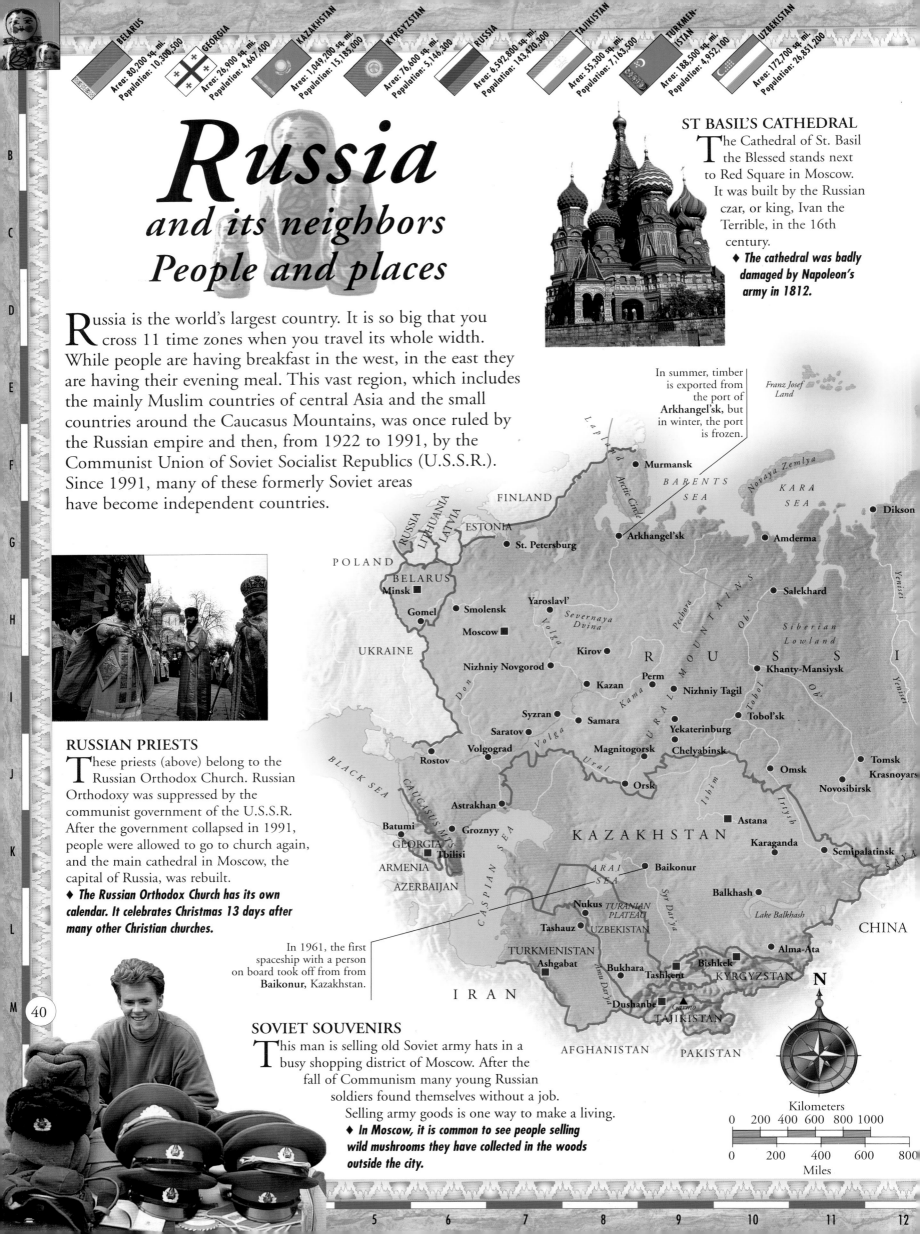

Franz Josef Land

Murmansk · BARENTS SEA · Novaya Zemlya · KARA SEA · Dikson

FINLAND · Arkhangel'sk · Amderma

RUSSIA · LITHUANIA · LATVIA · ESTONIA · St. Petersburg · Salekhard

POLAND · BELARUS · Minsk · Yaroslavl' · Severnaya Dvina · Siberian Lowland

Gomel · Smolensk · Moscow · Kirov · Khanty-Mansiysk

UKRAINE · Nizhniy Novgorod · Kazan · Perm · Nizhniy Tagil · Tobol'sk

Syzran · Samara · Yekaterinburg · Tomsk · Krasnoyars

Saratov · Magnitogorsk · Chelyabinsk · Omsk · Novosibirsk

Volgograd · Orsk

Rostov · BLACK SEA · Astrakhan · KAZAKHSTAN · Astana · Karaganda · Semipalatinsk

Batumi · Groznyy · Baikonur · Balkhash · Lake Balkhash

GEORGIA · Tbilisi · CASPIAN SEA · ARAL SEA · Syr Dar'ya · CHINA

ARMENIA · AZERBAIJAN · Nukus · TURANIAN PLATEAU · Alma-Ata

Tashauz · UZBEKISTAN · Bishkek

TURKMENISTAN · Ashgabat · Bukhara · Tashkent · KYRGYZSTAN

IRAN · Dushanbe · TAJIKISTAN

AFGHANISTAN · PAKISTAN

N

Kilometers
0 200 400 600 800 1000

0 200 400 600 800
Miles

MIR SPACE STATION

In 1971, the Soviet Union launched the first space station to orbit the Earth. In 1986, space station Mir (right) was launched with a crew of Russian astronauts.

♦ **U.S. space shuttles regularly visited Mir from 1995 to 1998.**

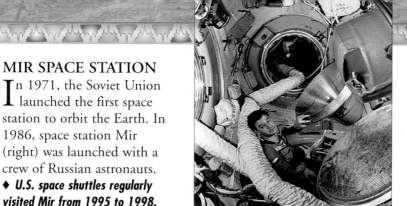

TRADITIONAL RUSSIA

Many Russian foods use grains and vegetables grown on the country's rich soils. Black rye bread is eaten at every meal, and small pancakes, called blinis, are served with the most prized delicacy, caviar — the tiny black eggs of the sturgeon fish. Soup is often eaten at lunch. A favorite is beet soup, called borscht, served with sour cream. Water for tea is heated in an urn called a samovar.

♦ **The balalaika is a Russian musical instrument invented in the 18th century, and Russian dolls are a traditional toy.**

Russian dolls

Tea

Borscht soup

Blinis with caviar

Black rye bread

Balalaika

Verkhoyansk is the coldest city in the world: a temperature of -95° F (-71° C) has been recorded.

Kamchatka has 22 active volcanoes. The largest is Klyuchevskaya.

SAMARKAND

Over the centuries, many people have conquered this ancient city in Uzbekistan, including Persians, Greeks, Arabs, Turks, and Russians. Samarkand was the capital of Tamerlane, a great warrior emperor who ruled from 1369 to 1405. Around Registan Square (right) in the old city, there are three madrasahs, or Islamic schools.

♦ **Tamerlane's armies rampaged across central Asia, from India to Turkey.**

The Trans-Siberian Railway passes through **Ulan-Ude**; the railway is 9,300 km (5,780 mi) long.

MONGOLIA

Map labels

Bering St.
BERING SEA
Arctic Circle
Os. Vrangelya
Anadyr'
ARCTIC OCEAN
EAST SIBERIAN SEA
Novosibirskiye Ostrova
Ernaya emlya
LAPTEV SEA
Os. Lyakhovskiy
Delta of the Lena
Kolyma
Kolyma Lowland
KOLYMA RANGE
KAMCHATKA
Klyuchevskaya
Nordvik
Indigirka
CHERSKOGO RANGE
Verkhoyansk
VERKHOYANSK RANGE
Lena
Magadan
DZHUGDZHUR RANGE
SEA OF OKHOTSK
ENTRAL IBERIAN LATEAU
Yakutsk
Sakhalin
Olekminsk
ALDANSKOYE NAGOR'YE
Nizhnyaya Tunguska
Lensk
Tatarskiy Proliv
STANOVOY RANGE
gara
YABLONOVYY RANGE
Amur
SIKHOTE-ALIN'
Bratsk
Lake Baikal
Kharbarovsk
Irkutsk
Ulan-Ude
niseí TS
Vladivostok

ST. PETERSBURG

Russia's second largest city was planned by Czar Peter I in 1703. He named the city after himself. The city has many fine buildings, including the Hermitage Museum (left) in the czar's Winter Palace.

♦ **St. Petersburg was called Petrograd and then Leningrad by the Soviet government. Now it is again called St. Petersburg.**

Data file

Area	8,242,179 sq. mi./21,347,100 sq km
Population	219 million
Independent countries	8
Largest country	Russia (6,592,800 sq. mi./17,075,400 sq km)
Smallest country	Georgia (26,900 sq. mi./69,700 sq km)
Most populated country	Russia (143,420,300)
Least populated country	Turkmenistan (4,952,100)
Largest cities	Moscow, Russia (8.7 million); St. Petersburg, Russia (4.8 million)
Highest mountain	Garmo (Communism Peak), Tajikistan (24,590 ft./7,495 m)
Longest rivers	Yenisei (3,449 mi./5,550 km); Ob-Irtysh (3,362 mi./5,411 km)
Largest lakes	Caspian Sea (143,241 sq. mi./370,992 sq km); Aral Sea (14,290 sq. mi./37,000 sq km)
Religions	Russian Orthodox, Muslim
Languages	Russian, national languages

Russia and its neighbors:
Nature, farming and industry

The natural landscapes of this region are strongly influenced by climate. They are arranged in huge bands stretching west to east. In the Arctic north, winters are bitterly cold and the soil is permanently frozen. Reindeer herders live there. To the south of this cold zone, there are vast coniferous forests, called taiga, where bears and wolves live. Below are the wide grasslands, called steppes, which are home to herds of grazing animals. Further south are dry lands and deserts, surrounding the inland waters of the Caspian and Aral Seas. Most Russians live in the European part of the region to the west of the Ural Mountains. Here the richer soils make good farmland, and the climate is less severe. Industries based on iron and coal grew around the Volga and Don river basins.

STREET MARKET

People in Russia and its neighboring countries like to buy their fruit and vegetables from open-air markets such as this one (above). The farmers come to the city each day to sell their produce.

♦ *Under the communist government of the Soviet Union, farmers did not own their land but had to work on large, state-owned farms.*

HERDERS OF THE NORTH

The northern parts of Russia are too cold to grow crops. So many people of the region, such as the Buryats, Yakuts, and Nentsi, make their living by herding reindeer or catching fish. These peole eat reindeer meat and make clothes from the animals' skins. This man (right) is from the Taz River region of western Siberia.

♦ *Siberia is rich in oil, natural gas, coal, iron, and gold. Although these resources are being developed, local people have been allowed to carry on a traditional way of life.*

SHRINKING SEA

The Aral Sea (left) lies between Uzbekistan and Kazakhstan, but it is fed by waters from Tajikistan, Kyrgyzstan, and Afghanistan. These countries are very dry, so they quarrel over scarce water. So much water has been taken from the rivers to irrigate cotton fields that, in recent years, the sea has shrunk drastically.

♦ *The Aral Sea's water level has fallen by 53 ft. (16 m) over the last 30 years, leaving ships stranded and rusting on the former lake bed.*

ON THE STEPPES

The steppes are a vast plain that stretches all the way from Ukraine to Siberia. These sweeping grasslands are bordered by woods to the north and by desert to the south. The climate is generally too cold in winter and too hot and dry in summer for trees to survive. Grasses, such as feather grass and needle grass, have deep roots that can tap water from under the ground. This helps them withstand the drought.

♦ *The saiga lives on the steppes. Its large nose has hair-lined passages to warm up the air and filter out dust.*

Saiga

Sandgrouse

Hamster

Great bustard

Feather grass

OIL PIPELINE

Huge oil reserves have been found in western Siberia, in the Ural-Volga region and around the Caspian Sea. To get the oil to distant cities, long pipelines were built (right), often in remote places and in the bitter cold of winter.

♦ **Russia has 39,000 mi. (63,000 km) of oil pipelines.**

FARMING REGIONS

Although this is a vast region, much of the land is not good for farming. The north is too cold, the south too hot, and other regions are too far from markets and consumers. The best farmland is found after forests have been cut down, exposing chernozem, the black earth, which supports big wheat fields. In desert regions, irrigation makes it possible to grow cotton and rice.

Many farms in western Russia specialize in cabbages and root crops.

Around Moscow is an area of market gardening.

In the far east it is hot and rainy enough to grow vegetables, rice, and fruit.

River water is diverted from the Aral Sea to irrigate cotton fields.

Herds of sheep, goats, camels, and horses graze on the dry lands of Central Asia.

▨	Reindeer
▨	Dairy
▨	Grain, crops & livestock
▨	Sheep, goats & camels
▨	Fruit
▨	Cotton

CHANGING WAYS

Under the Communist system, the government of the Soviet Union ran most factories and farms. This meant that people's basic needs of food, clothing, and housing were met, and rents were low. Luxuries, however, especially from abroad, were almost impossible to get. When the U.S. fast-food chain McDonald's opened its first restaurant in Moscow in 1990, people stood in line for hours.

♦ **Under its last communist leader, Mikhail Gorbachev, the government started to allow foreign companies to invest in the country.**

Osprey

Sable

Baikal seal

LAKE BAIKAL

Lake Baikal, which is 5,315 ft. (1,620 m), deep, is the deepest lake in the world. Many species of animals, including 52 kinds of fish and 250 different types of shrimp, are found nowhere else in the world. The Baikal seal is the world's smallest and only freshwater seal. The females give birth to their babies in early spring in lairs under breathing holes in the snow.

♦ **Lake Baikal has 336 rivers flowing into it, but it has just one outlet, the River Angara.**

ARMENIA — Area: 11,500 sq. mi. Population: 2,982,900
AZERBAIJAN — Area: 33,400 sq. mi. Population: 7,912,000
BAHRAIN — Area: 267 sq. mi. Population: 668,300
CYPRUS — Area: 3,572 sq. mi. Population: 780,100
IRAN — Area: 634,559 sq. mi. Population: 68,017,900
IRAQ — Area: 169,235 sq. mi. Population: 26,074,900
ISRAEL — Area: 7,992 sq. mi. Population: 6,726,900
JORDAN — Area: 34,443 sq. mi. Population: 5,759,700
KUWAIT — Area: 6,880 sq. mi. Population: 2,335,600

South West Asia
People and places

South West Asia, also often called the Middle East, lies at the junction of three continents: Africa, Asia, and Europe. This region has been very important throughout history. Ancient cultures such as the Sumerian and Persian civilizations thrived in Mesopotamia, the area between the Tigris and Euphrates Rivers. These civilizations developed writing about 4000 B.C. and the plow about 3500 B.C. Later, the religions of Judaism, Christianity, and Islam began in the region. Today, Jerusalem and Mecca are major centers of religious pilgrimage and worship. For centuries, nomads have herded animals across the dry lands. Today, more and more people from rural areas are moving to the region's thriving modern cities.

TRADITIONAL CURE

This Turkish woman (right) is having a traditional treatment for arthritis. Her inflamed joints are soothed by being buried in sand. The leaves protect her head from the heat of the sun.

♦ *Turkey is a rapidly developing country, but many traditional ways continue.*

The bridges across the Bosporus Strait in **Istanbul** connect Europe with Asia.

BEDOUIN NOMADS

The Bedouin are traditionally nomadic and are a proud and independent people. They used to wander across deserts, moving their herds of sheep, goats, and cattle from one sparse pasture to another. Their most prized animal is the camel, which provides milk and meat and can carry heavy loads. Camels have been known to go for many months without water.

♦ *There are about one million Bedouin in South West Asia. Today, many have permanently settled as farmers.*

PETRA

The ancient city of Petra, in Jordan, was carved out of sandstone rock in about 1000 B.C. by the Edomites. In 312 B.C., it became the capital of the Nabateans, who were Arab nomads. After an earthquake in A.D. 551, the city was left in ruins and deserted. Striking facades cut into the rock and numerous cave dwellings are all that remains.

♦ *Petra is approached through a narrow passage between cliffs. It was rediscovered in 1812 by a Swiss traveller disguised as an Arab.*

MECCA

The prophet Mohammed was born in Mecca, now in Saudi Arabia, in A.D. 570. Mecca is one of Islam's holiest places, and every year two million worshippers travel to the Great Mosque (right) on a pilgrimage called the *hajj*.

♦ *There are more than one thousand million Muslims in the world.*

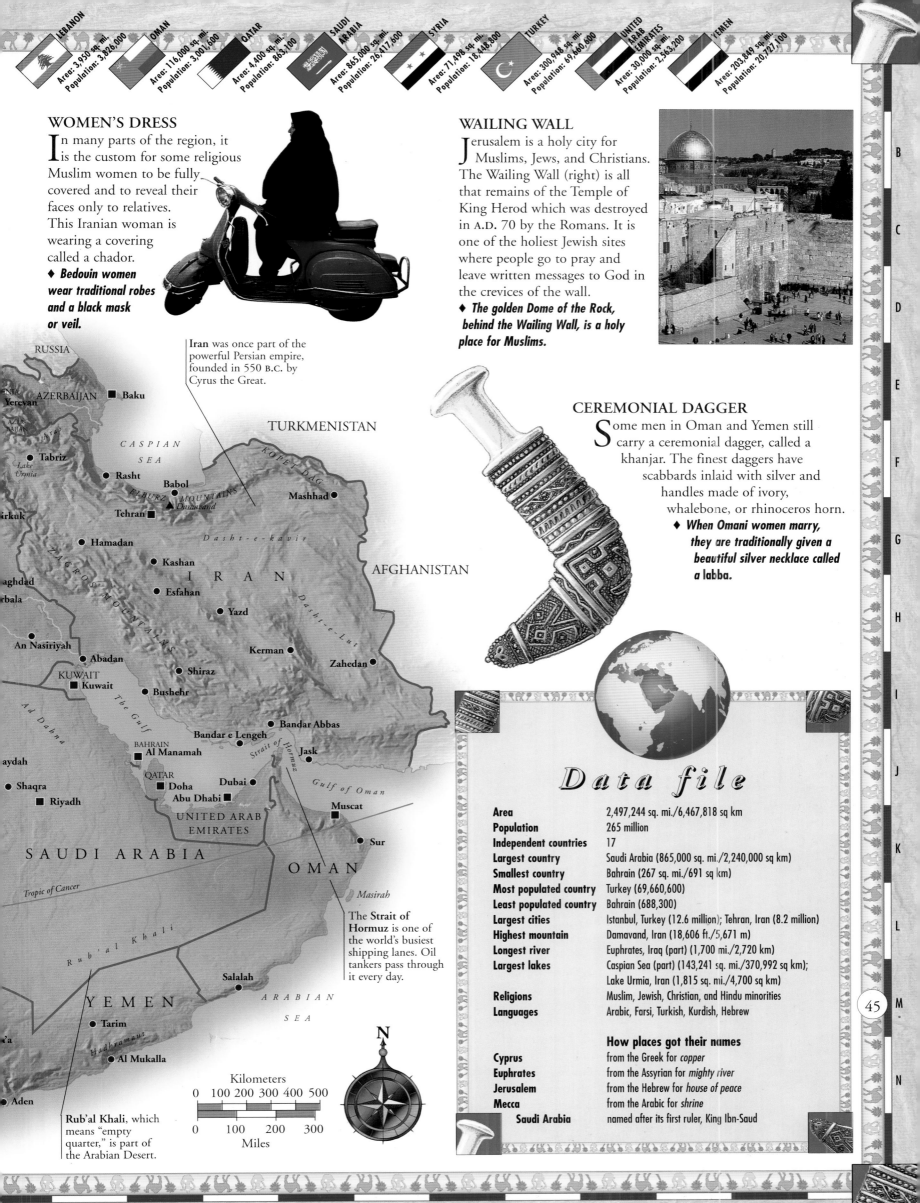

WOMEN'S DRESS

In many parts of the region, it is the custom for some religious Muslim women to be fully covered and to reveal their faces only to relatives. This Iranian woman is wearing a covering called a chador.

♦ **Bedouin women wear traditional robes and a black mask or veil.**

WAILING WALL

Jerusalem is a holy city for Muslims, Jews, and Christians. The Wailing Wall (right) is all that remains of the Temple of King Herod which was destroyed in A.D. 70 by the Romans. It is one of the holiest Jewish sites where people go to pray and leave written messages to God in the crevices of the wall.

♦ **The golden Dome of the Rock, behind the Wailing Wall, is a holy place for Muslims.**

Iran was once part of the powerful Persian empire, founded in 550 B.C. by Cyrus the Great.

CEREMONIAL DAGGER

Some men in Oman and Yemen still carry a ceremonial dagger, called a khanjar. The finest daggers have scabbards inlaid with silver and handles made of ivory, whalebone, or rhinoceros horn.

♦ **When Omani women marry, they are traditionally given a beautiful silver necklace called a labba.**

RUSSIA

AZERBAIJAN
Yerevan
Baku
AZER BAIJAN
Tabriz
Lake Urmia

CASPIAN SEA

TURKMENISTAN

KOPET DAG

Rasht
ELBURZ MOUNTAINS
Babol
Damavand
Mashhad
Tehran
Hamadan

Dasht-e-kavir

AFGHANISTAN

ZAGROS MOUNTAINS

irkuk
aghdad
rbala

Kashan
I R A N
Esfahan
Yazd

Dasht-e-Lut

An Nasiriyah
Abadan
Kerman
Zahedan
KUWAIT
Shiraz
Kuwait

Ad Dahna
The Gulf
Bushehr
Bandar Abbas
Bandar e Lengeh
BAHRAIN
Al Manamah
Strait of Hormuz
Jask
aydah
QATAR
Shaqra
Doha
Dubai
Gulf of Oman
Riyadh
Abu Dhabi
UNITED ARAB EMIRATES
Muscat
SAUDI ARABIA
O M A N
Sur
Tropic of Cancer
Masirah

The **Strait of Hormuz** is one of the world's busiest shipping lanes. Oil tankers pass through it every day.

Rub'al Khali
Salalah
ARABIAN SEA

Y E M E N
Tarim
Hadhramaut
a
Al Mukalla
Aden

Rub'al Khali, which means "empty quarter," is part of the Arabian Desert.

Kilometers
0 100 200 300 400 500

0 100 200 300
Miles

N

Data file

Area	2,497,244 sq. mi./6,467,818 sq km
Population	265 million
Independent countries	17
Largest country	Saudi Arabia (865,000 sq. mi./2,240,000 sq km)
Smallest country	Bahrain (267 sq. mi./691 sq km)
Most populated country	Turkey (69,660,600)
Least populated country	Bahrain (688,300)
Largest cities	Istanbul, Turkey (12.6 million); Tehran, Iran (8.2 million)
Highest mountain	Damavand, Iran (18,606 ft./5,671 m)
Longest river	Euphrates, Iraq (part) (1,700 mi./2,720 km)
Largest lakes	Caspian Sea (part) (143,241 sq. mi./370,992 sq km); Lake Urmia, Iran (1,815 sq. mi./4,700 sq km)
Religions	Muslim, Jewish, Christian, and Hindu minorities
Languages	Arabic, Farsi, Turkish, Kurdish, Hebrew

How places got their names

Cyprus	from the Greek for copper
Euphrates	from the Assyrian for mighty river
Jerusalem	from the Hebrew for house of peace
Mecca	from the Arabic for shrine
Saudi Arabia	named after its first ruler, King Ibn-Saud

South West Asia:
Nature, farming, and industry

South West Asia is a region dominated by mountains and deserts. Animals and plants have developed strategies for surviving in these harsh environments. People have also learned to adapt by sinking wells to reach underground water and by building canals to irrigate the land. Along the Gulf coast, there are many desalination plants, where salty seawater is treated and turned into fresh water for drinking. In other places, new irrigation methods have brought desert areas to life. In more recent times, oil has joined water as a vital resource. It has brought enormous wealth to countries such as Saudi Arabia, Kuwait, Bahrain, Qatar, and the United Arab Emirates.

HERDING GOATS

Where the land is too dry for planting crops, people graze animals such as sheep, goats, and cattle. These animals were first domesticated in South West Asia over 7,000 years ago. This Kurdish goatherd (right) is watching over his animals in eastern Turkey.

♦ *In Turkey and Iran, there are more sheep and goats than people.*

WILD FLOWERS

The ancient Babylonians and Assyrians were famed for their gardens, which were full of ornamental plants, palm trees, and ponds. The Hanging Gardens of Babylon were one of the Seven Wonders of the Ancient World. Flowers, such as the lily, lotus, and rose, were prized. Popular garden plants of today originally from South West Asia include irises, crocuses, and tulips (above: left, center, and right).

♦ *Turkey exports flower bulbs around the world, but protects its rare flowers in reserves.*

Scorpion

Jerboa

DATE PALM

Date palms are ideally suited to dry conditions because their long roots tap water deep underground. After the dates have been picked, they are dried and packed for export abroad. The trunk of the date palm is used for lumber and making furniture.

♦ *Iran, Saudi Arabia, and Iraq together produce almost half the world's dates.*

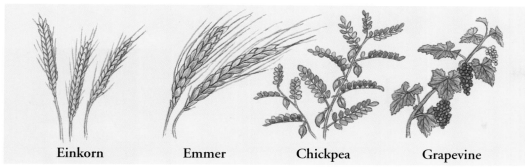

Einkorn **Emmer** **Chickpea** **Grapevine**

REGIONAL CROPS

Around 8000 B.C., the ancient peoples of Sumeria, which is now Iraq, planted crops from seeds and stored grain after harvest. The Sumerians were the world's first farmers.

♦ *All the world's different varieties of wheat originally came from ancient grasses such as einkorn and emmer.*

OILFIELDS

South West Asia is the world's most important oil region. About 60 percent of all the world's crude oil is found there. Oil comes from the remains of sea animals buried and crushed in layers of rock and sand many years ago. People first used oil, which they found in places where it surfaces naturally, for sealing ships' hulls to make them waterproof. In the 20th century, drills were invented that reach oil deep underground. Usually, oil reserves are found at least 490 ft. (150 m) down, and they are often found together with natural gas. Sometimes, the gas is burned off, producing flares such as these (left).

♦ *Saudi Arabia is the world's biggest oil-producing country. The United Arab Emirates is also a major oil producer.*

ARABIAN ORYX

This species of long-horned antelope was once found throughout the deserts of Arabia, including the Empty Quarter of Saudi Arabia, but it died out in its natural habitat in 1972. Fortunately, some Arabian oryxes were kept in zoos, and these animals were later reintroduced to the desert of Oman.

♦ *The oryx's pale coat reflects the sun's heat, and its splayed hooves allow it to walk easily on sand.*

Sinai leopard

Dung beetle

LIFE AMONG THE DUNES

The region's deserts include some of the most inhospitable places on Earth. The Empty Quarter in Saudi Arabia is a sea of sand dunes, with scorching heat and hardly any rainfall. There are also scrub deserts, with dry, rock-strewn ground and a few bushes. Deserts appear empty of life by day, but at night, sand cats, the rare Sinai leopard, jerboas, and scorpions come out to look for food. Oases are fertile patches in the desert where water reaches the surface.

♦ *Scorpions are hunters with powerful, pincer-like claws and stingers in their tails. The mother scorpion carries her tiny young on her back.*

FARMING IN ISRAEL

Israel has only small areas of fertile land. In the Negev Desert (above), people are careful with every drop of water. Farmers lay plastic tubes across fields to deliver water directly to the roots of each plant. They grow vegetables under plastic sheets in winter.

♦ *Israel produces over 90 percent of the food it needs with its efficient farming techniques. The country also exports oranges, grapefruit, and lemons.*

Southern *Asia*
People and places

There is enormous variety in the religious beliefs, customs, diet, dress, and languages of the people of Southern Asia. About 70 percent of the population live in the countryside, following a traditional way of life. There are nomadic herders in the mountains, farming villages on the plains, and fishing communities on the coasts. Large and fast-growing cities, such as Mumbai, Karachi, and Dhaka are home to millions of people. Religion plays an important part in people's lives. Afghanistan, Bangladesh, and Pakistan are primarily Muslim countries, while Bhutan is Buddhist. Nepal has people of both Hindu and Buddhist religions, and in India there are people of the Hindu, Muslim, Sikh, Christian, Buddhist, and Jain faiths.

STREET BUSINESS

Towns throughout the region usually include an old quarter of narrow streets and alleys, filled with houses, shops, and workshops. People often work from their homes, such as this dentist in Peshawar, Pakistan (right), or they run small businesses from street stalls. Crowds of people, cars, bicycle rickshaws, dogs, and other animals fill the streets.
♦ **Peshawar is in Pakistan's northwest frontier region, at the foot of the Khyber Pass.**

TEMPLE OFFERINGS

India is famous for its many spectacular temples. At a temple in a small town in India, these Jain priests (right) are making an offering to the giant statue of their saint, Bahubali. Jains will harm no living thing, even insects. Hindus have household shrines where they pray daily, as well as magnificent temples and small roadside shrines. Hindus offer colored powders, rice, flowers, and incense to their gods.
♦ **Many Hindus go on a pilgrimage to the holy city of Varanasi on the Ganges.**

HOLY MAN

Four out of every five Indians follow the Hindu religion. Hindus believe that the souls of living things never die, but are always reborn. Good deeds may be rewarded and bad deeds punished in the next life. Wandering holy men, called *sadhus* (right), meditate and live simple lives.
♦ **A sadhu lives with few belongings — a simple garment, staff, begging bowl, and water pot.**

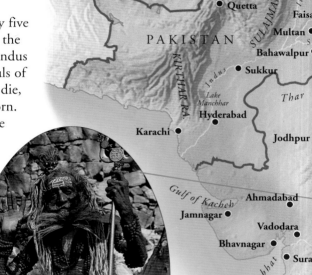

BUDDHA'S SACRED TOOTH

Every year, the Sri Lankan town of Kandy holds a festival and a great procession. A tooth, believed to be from Siddhartha Gautama, the Buddha, is taken from its shrine and carried through the streets by elephant.
♦ **Siddhartha was the Indian prince and spiritual teacher who founded Buddhism.**

GOLDEN TEMPLE

Guru Nanak founded the Sikh religion in the 15th century. There are now about 20 million Sikhs, mostly in northern India but also in communities around the world. The Golden Temple at Amritsar, in the Punjab region of India (below), is the holiest Sikh shrine.
♦ **Sikh men traditionally do not cut their hair and they wear a turban.**

TURKMENISTAN

Mazar-e Sharif

Herat

HINDU KUSH

AFGHANISTAN

Kabul

Khyber Pass

IRAN

Pesh

Kandahar

Quetta

Faisala

Multan

Su

PAKISTAN

SULAIMAN RANGE

Bahawalpur

KIRTHAR RA

Indus

Sukkur

Lake Manchhar

Thar D

Hyderabad

Karachi

Jodhpur

Gulf of Kacheh

Ahmadabad

Jamnagar

Vadodara

Bhavnagar

Surat

Gulf of Khambhat

Gulf of Khambhat

Mumbai (Bombay)

Pune

Sol

W E S T E R N

Kolha

Hub Dha

Mangalore

G H A T S

Coimbat

Cochin

Trivandru

Cape Como

INDIAN OCEAN

MALDIVES

TAJ MAHAL

The beautiful Taj Mahal stands in the Indian city of Agra, on the banks of the Yamuna River. It was built by the Mogul emperor, Shah Jahan, as a tomb for his wife. Construction began about 1630, and it took 20,000 workers 20 years to build the Taj Mahal. They created a gleaming, white marble building, topped by a magnificent dome and surrounded by four tall, narrow minarets. Skilled artisans carved intricate designs into the marble. Others laid out gardens and a narrow pool, which reflects the dome in its waters. Shah Jahan was later buried beside his wife inside the monument he left to the world.

♦ **The Mogul emperors were Muslims who ruled India from 1526 to 1858.**

DYE STALL

Indians use natural dyes to color cloth, prepare foods, and make colored water and powder for festivals. This man is selling dyes in a market in southern India.

♦ **The root of the madder plant gives red dye, and yellow saffron comes from the crocus flower.**

SHERPAS

Sherpas are farmers, herders, and traders who live in the mountains of Nepal. Expeditions climbing the Himalayan peaks hire Sherpas as skilled mountaineers, guides, and bearers capable of carrying heavy loads.

♦ **Sherpas live in some of the highest villages in the world.**

Thimphu, the capital of Bhutan, lies high in the Himalayas at an altitude of 8,038 ft. (2,450 m).

Silt carried by the **Ganges** and **Brahmaputra** rivers creates fertile farmland around the Bay of Bengal.

The Deccan Plateau, in southern central India, was formed by a giant sheet of volcanic lava.

N

Kilometers
0 100 200 300 400 500

0   100   200   300
Miles

Data file

Area	1,984,438 sq. mi./5,139,660 sq km
Population	1,533 million
Independent countries	8
Largest country	India (1,269,219 sq. mi./3,287,263 sq km)
Smallest country	Maldives (115 sq. mi./288 sq km)
Most populated country	India (1,080,264,400)
Least populated country	Maldives (349,100)
Largest cities	Mumbai, India (18 million); Calcutta, India (12.9 million)
Highest mountain	Mount Everest, Nepal/China (29,035 ft./8,850 m)
Longest river	Indus, Pakistan (1,800 mi./2,900 km)
Largest lake	Manchhar, Pakistan (100 sq. mi./260 sq km)
Religions	Hindu, Muslim, Buddhist, Sikh
Languages	Hindi, English, Bengali, Marathi, Gujarati, Assamese, Punjabi, Urdu, Pashto, Nepali, Dzongkha, Sinhala

How places got their names

Mount Everest	after Sir George Everest (1790–1866), surveyor-general of India
Himalayas	from the Sanskrit for *abode of the snow*

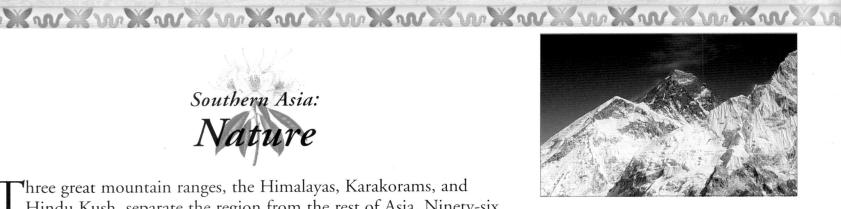

Southern Asia:
Nature

Three great mountain ranges, the Himalayas, Karakorams, and Hindu Kush, separate the region from the rest of Asia. Ninety-six of the world's tallest peaks, including the highest of all, Mount Everest, are found in these mountains. Melting snow in the highlands feeds huge rivers, such as the Indus, Ganges, and Brahmaputra. Some of the world's first cities and civilizations were built on the lower plains beside their waters. The area where the Ganges and Brahmaputra enter the Indian Ocean forms a low-lying delta region of shifting river channels and mangrove swamps. Central India was once covered in tropical forests, which were home to elephants, tigers, and monkeys. Today, much of the forest has been cleared to make way for farms.

MOUNT EVEREST

The highest mountain peak in the world, Mount Everest, is over 4.9 mi. (8 km) above sea level. Everest lies on the border between Nepal and Tibet (China). The first people to conquer the steep, icy slopes and reach the summit were a New Zealander, Edmund Hillary, and a Nepali Sherpa, Tenzing Norgay, in 1953.
♦ *The mountain's Tibetan name is* Chomolungma, *meaning "mother goddess of the earth."*

Snow leopard • Himalayan tahr • Lammergeier • Marmot

MOUNTAIN WILDLIFE

Many different animals live in the forests of the Himalayan foothills, while others survive on the rocky slopes above the trees. The snow leopard has fur on the thick pads of its paws, helping it to grip the ice. Sheep and goats feed on vegetation among the rocks, and the goatlike Himalayan tahr lives on steep, tree-covered mountain slopes.
♦ *The lammergeier drops the bones of its prey onto rocks. The bones split open, and the bird feeds on the bone marrow.*

LANGURS

Although primarily forest monkeys, langurs (below) are also found in many towns and temple grounds. Because Hindus consider them to be sacred animals, they are never harmed and are often fed by people.
♦ *Hindus regard some langurs as the spirit of the legendary Hanuman, a kindly monkey king.*

Rhododendron · Agapetes (a heather relative)

HIMALAYAN FLOWERS

The Himalayas are rich in plant life. There are rare and beautiful orchids, and flowering shrubs, such as rhododendrons and magnolias. These plants are now found in gardens around the world.
♦ *The name rhododendron means "rose tree."*

DESERT FESTIVAL

The town of Pushkar, in the Indian state of Rajasthan, holds an annual festival that combines religious worship with a huge livestock fair. Herders come from all over the region to sell their camels and cattle (right). There are camel races and plenty of singing and dancing. The festival has become a popular tourist attraction.

♦ *Camels are ideally suited to Rajasthan's desert conditions because they can go for months without drinking any water.*

MANGROVE SWAMP

The delta formed by the Ganges and Brahmaputra rivers, in Bangladesh and northeast India, contains the biggest mangrove swamp in the world, called the Sundarbans. Mangrove trees grow on flat, muddy ground on tropical coasts. They have adapted to living where salty seawater and fresh river water meet. Some have developed vertical extensions on the roots that are exposed at low tide and allow the plants to breathe. The swamp is home to the rare Sundarbans tiger, which preys on spotted, or chital, deer.

♦ *The mouths of the Ganges and Brahmaputra rivers form the largest delta in the world.*

RAJASTHAN PLAINS

Many years ago, Rajasthan (below) was covered in forest. Today, few trees remain except in protected areas, such as the Ranthambor National Park, a sanctuary for tigers. The forests have been chopped down to make way for farmland or to provide people with fuel for heating and cooking. In this dry desert and semidesert climate, drought is often a problem. Irrigation canals have been built so that crops, such as millet, sorghum, and wheat, can be grown. The biggest canal is the Indira Gandhi canal, which brings water from rivers in the north.

♦ *Ancient, fossilized tree trunks can be found on the surface of the Thar Desert, in Rajasthan.*

Chital deer

Mangrove tree root extensions

THE COBRA AND THE MONGOOSE

Cobras are poisonous snakes that can be up to 18 ft. (5.5 m) long. To scare attackers, a cobra rears up and spreads out the skin around its neck. Its unlikely enemy is the Indian mongoose, which measures just 10 in. (25 cm) long. Fast and alert, it can dodge the snake's fangs and jump in with a killing bite to the neck.

♦ *The Indian mongoose is sometimes kept as a pet to rid people's homes of rats, mice, and snakes.*

Sundarbans tiger

Scarlet ibis

Southern Asia:
Farming and industry

Two out of every three people in Southern Asia make their living from raising crops or keeping animals. Almost everyone in Afghanistan, Nepal, and Bhutan lives off the land. India and Pakistan's rapidly growing cities are home to new, growing industries and millions of people. These countries export textiles, machines, and computers to the rest of the world. Throughout Southern Asia, making crafts is an important small industry. Carpets, leather, jewelry, copperware, and wooden goods are both sold to tourists and exported to other countries.

MUMBAI

Mumbai, previously called Bombay, is one of India's great cities. It was originally built on islands in a swamp. Because it has the best harbor on the west coast, Portuguese and British traders settled in Mumbai. Later, it became the commercial and industrial heart of India, with factories making textiles, clothes, bicycles, and other goods. A quarter of India's manufactured goods are made in Mumbai. Millions of people from the countryside have come to the city. The city is so overcrowded that many people live in slums.

♦ *Mumbai is the center of India's large film industry. Indians all over the world can watch films that were made in "Bollywood."*

SPICE MARKET

In the wetter regions of Southern Asia, people eat a lot of rice, while in drier areas, they make flat naan and chapatti bread from wheat or millet. Most meals are simple. Common dishes include dal, a kind of porridge made from lentils and beans, cooked vegetables, and yogurt. Meat is rarely eaten by most people. Following the rules of their religion, Muslims do not eat pork, and Hindus do not eat beef. Dishes are subtly flavored with all kinds of spices and tend to be hotter in the south. Spices include cardamom, turmeric, pepper, cloves, and cumin. People buy their spices from open-air markets, such as this one in Jaipur, India (right).

♦ *The Arabian Sea coast of the Indian state of Kerala was known to merchants as the Spice Coast because of its wealth of spices.*

STILT FISHING

In many coastal villages throughout Southern Asia, fishing is an important way of life. Some traditional fishing methods have remained unchanged for centuries. In Kerala, in southwest India, a big net is stretched between the beach and a boat, and bands of people help drag the net back to shore. In Sri Lanka, men perch on stilts driven into the sea bed (above) and fish with a rod and line. The positions of the stilts are highly valued and are passed on from father to son.

♦ *Fishing is the most important industry in the Maldives, an island chain in the Indian Ocean. It employs a quarter of all workers. There are over a thousand kinds of local fish.*

SHIP-BREAKING

Although Southern Asia has many huge industries, there are also thousands of smaller workshops and factories throughout the region. Many of these enterprises use recycled materials and recondition unwanted goods. Nothing is allowed to go to waste. The shipbuilding industry is an example of recycling on a large scale. At Chittagong, in Bangladesh, old ships are broken down into scrap (above left) to supply iron, steel, electrical parts, and anything else that can be salvaged. On a smaller scale, some people in towns and cities recover glass, metal, and paper from garbage dumps for recycling.

♦ *As well as being the country's main port, Chittagong is a major industrial center of Bangladesh. It has jute mills, textile factories, engineering works, and oil refineries.*

WORKING ELEPHANTS

Many of Southern Asia's forests are in hilly regions that vehicles cannot reach. Foresters often use elephants to shift logs and carry heavy loads. The young elephants are trained by their handlers, called *mahouts*, to use their trunk and tusks to lift heavy logs. An elephant's trunk is flexible and strong. It has over 40,000 muscles along its length. Elephants were also once used to carry hunters through the forest and troops into battle.

♦ *Asian elephants are still found in the wild in India's Assam and West Bengal regions, and in Bangladesh.*

FARMING REGIONS

Crops and farming in Southern Asia vary according to climate. Rice fields, called paddies, are found in areas that receive heavy monsoon rains. In the northern plains of India and Pakistan, where the Indus and Ganges rivers provide irrigation, farmers grow wheat and millet. In the dry lands of Afghanistan and Pakistan, cotton is the main crop. In the mountain regions of the Himalayas, nomads herd yaks, goats, and sheep.

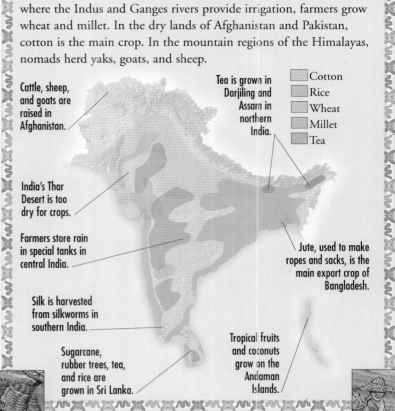

Cattle, sheep, and goats are raised in Afghanistan.

Tea is grown in Darjiling and Assam in northern India.

Cotton
Rice
Wheat
Millet
Tea

India's Thar Desert is too dry for crops.

Farmers store rain in special tanks in central India.

Jute, used to make ropes and sacks, is the main export crop of Bangladesh.

Silk is harvested from silkworms in southern India.

Tropical fruits and coconuts grow on the Andaman Islands.

Sugarcane, rubber trees, tea, and rice are grown in Sri Lanka.

TEA HARVEST

Tea comes from a shrub native to Asia. It grows best in areas of high rainfall and at altitudes of 3,300 to 6,600 ft. (1,000 to 2,000 m). India's Assam region, northern Bangladesh, and Sri Lanka are some of the world's main tea-growing regions. Only the buds and smallest leaves are picked from the bushes.

♦ *People have been drinking tea for at least 4,000 years, and it is the world's most popular hot drink.*

MODERN TECHNOLOGY

India is a country of farms and villages, but it also has a rapidly growing industrial economy. Heavy industries, such as iron and steel, are found in Bihar, West Bengal, and Orissa. India's plentiful coal supplies fuel these industries. The country also has advanced high-tech companies building airplanes, rockets, and satellites. The center of India's growing computer industry is the city of Bangalore, where these workers (left) are writing software programs. Hundreds of other factories make less expensive goods, such as bicycles and sewing machines.

♦ *In India, many automobiles are made from designs licensed by foreign companies.*

BRUNEI	CAMBODIA	INDONESIA	LAOS	MALAYSIA	MYANMAR	PALAU	PAPUA NEW GUINEA	PHILIPPINES
Area: 2,226 sq. mi. Population: 372,400	Area: 69,898 sq. mi. Population: 13,607,100	Area: 741,103 sq. mi. Population: 241,973,900	Area: 91,400 sq. mi. Population: 6,217,100	Area: 127,584 sq. mi. Population: 23,953,100	Area: 261,228 sq. mi. Population: 42,909,500	Area: 177 sq. mi. Population: 20,300	Area: 178,703 sq. mi. Population: 5,545,300	Area: 115,800 sq. mi. Population: 87,857,500

South East Asia
People and places

Tropical South East Asia is made up of thousands of islands and peninsulas. The largest country, Indonesia, has more than 13,000 islands. The peoples of South East Asia have a long history of trading with each other and with the rest of the world. As a result, the thriving modern cities, such as Djakarta, Singapore, and Kuala Lumpur, are a rich mix of cultures, languages, and economies. The South East Asian countries have people of Islamic, Buddhist, Hindu, and Christian faiths.

VILLAGE LIFE

Some forest-dwellers in Malaysia and Indonesia still live in their traditional way, in large wooden longhouses. As many as 60 families may live together under one roof. The houses may be more than 650 ft. (200 m) long.
♦ *The longhouse has a communal porch and an attic where the villagers store their grain.*

ANGKOR WAT

This Hindu temple (left), in the jungle of Cambodia, is part of Angkor Wat, the largest complex of religious buildings in the world. The temple was built in the 12th century.
♦ *Angkor Wat means "Temple City."*

FLOATING MARKET

In much of densely forested South East Asia, waterways are the main link between villages. Thailand is famous for its floating markets. Boats, called sampans (right), carry fresh tomatoes, limes, cauliflowers, chillies, and other produce along Thailand's rivers and the canals of its capital, Bangkok.
♦ *Thai food includes long-grained rice dishes cooked with vegetables and spices.*

STILT HOUSES

In the remote highlands of South East Asia, many people live in villages close to water. This one (right) is in Indonesia. The houses are built on stilts to escape floods caused by the monsoon rains.
♦ *Forest villagers grow crops and collect spices, fruits, and other tree produce from the jungle.*

SINGAPORE
Area: 240 sq. mi.
Population: 4,425,700

THAILAND
Area: 198,115 sq. mi.
Population: 65,444,400

VIETNAM
Area: 128,052 sq. mi.
Population: 83,535,600

EAST TIMOR
Area: 5,794 sq. mi.
Population: 1,040,900

SINGAPORE

Singapore, at the tip of the Malay peninsula, is one of the smallest and most prosperous countries in the world. Its wealth comes from its busy port, oil refineries, banking, international trading companies, and tourism.

♦ **The name Singapore means "lion city."**

The 7,107 islands of the **Philippines** are of volcanic origin. In 1991 Mount Pinatubo erupted, destroying the homes of 200,000 people.

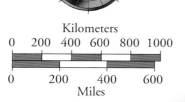

N

Kilometers
0   200   400   600   800   1000

0   200   400   600
Miles

PETRONAS TOWERS

These twin office towers in Kuala Lumpur, the capital of Malaysia, form the world's 4th tallest building. The Petronas Towers are 1,483 ft. (452 m) high. At the 50th of their 88 floors, the towers are joined by a glass-covered bridge. The Malaysian government built the towers to show the world how advanced the country has become.

♦ **Kuala Lumpur is a modern city where mosques and temples stand alongside freeways and skyscrapers.**

BALINESE DANCER

On the Indonesian island of Bali, people practice a traditional dance style that includes precise movements of the fingers and head.

♦ **Balinese culture is influenced by the Hindu religion.**

PALAU
■ Koror

PACIFIC OCEAN

Bougainville

New Britain

Jayapura ●

PAPUA NEW GUINEA

▲ *Puncak Jaya*

New Guinea

Port Moresby ■

Over 700 different local languages are spoken by the tribes of **Papua New Guinea.**

NDA SEA

A S I A

EAST TIMOR

SHWE DAGON PAGODA

According to legend, the Shwe Dagon Pagoda, a Buddhist temple in the city of Rangoon, Myanmar (right), contains relics of the Buddha. It is Myanmar's holiest shrine and is covered in gold and inlaid with colorful precious stones.

♦ **Shwe Dagon's bell-shaped dome, or stupa, is 325 ft. (99 m) high.**

Data file

Area	1,914,588 sq. mi./4,958,750 sq km
Population	574 million
Independent countries	13
Largest country	Indonesia (741,103 sq. mi./1,919,443 sq km)
Smallest country	Palau (177 sq. mi./458 sq km)
Most populated country	Indonesia (241,973,900)
Least populated country	Palau (20,300)
Largest cities	Manila, Philipines (10.8 million); Djakarta, Indonesia (8.7 million); Bangkok, Thailand (7.3 million);
Highest mountain	Puncak Jaya, Indonesia (16,502 ft./5,039 m)
Longest river	Mekong, Laos/Cambodia/Vietnam (2,597 mi./4,180 km)
Largest lake	Tonle Sap, Cambodia (3,860 sq. mi./10,000 sq km, in the wet season)
Religions	Muslim, Buddhist, Christian, Hindu
Languages	National and other regional languages
How places got their names	
Bangkok	from the Thai for *village of the wild plum*
Cambodia	from Cambu, the ancestors of the Khmers (the people of Cambodia)
Kuala Lumpur	from the Malay for *muddy river mouth*
Philippines	after King Philip II of Spain
Vietnam	from the Vietnamese for *land of the south*

B C D E F G H I J K L M N

South East Asia:
Nature, farming, and industry

South East Asia is rich in natural resources, such as timber, oil, gold, tin, and rubber. These resources have enabled countries, such as Malaysia, Singapore, and Indonesia, to grow and develop. Other countries, such as Laos and Papua New Guinea, have not yet fully exploited their resources. South East Asia's forests, mangrove swamps, and surrounding seas are home to a huge variety of wildlife. Many plants and animals are under threat from logging, dam-building, and clearing land for farming.

FOREST ANIMALS AND PLANTS

The tropical rain forests of South East Asia are rich in plant and animal species, especially on New Guinea and the Indonesian island of Borneo, which have been less disturbed by humans. Strange and unique plants include the giant, parasitic rafflesia, the world's largest flower, and the insect-eating pitcher plant.

♦ *The proboscis monkey, found in Borneo, gets its name from its long nose.*

Green python

Lar gibbon

OIL AND GAS

Some South East Asian countries have enough oil and natural gas to supply their own needs and to export abroad. Oil is extracted on land in Indonesia and Malaysia, and offshore in the Gulf of Thailand.

♦ *Singapore is a major center of oil refining.*

Proboscis monkey

Tree shrew

Prince Rudolph's blue

Enameled

White-plumed

Little king

BIRDS OF PARADISE

There are 49 species of these amazing, colorful birds (left). Almost all of them are found only on the island of New Guinea. They all have fantastic feathers, including fans, plumes, and tail streamers up to 24 in. (60 cm) long. The male birds show off these feathers in their courtship displays.

♦ *The dramatic display of plumage by male birds of paradise is often accompanied by calls that sound like the crack of a whip.*

MODERN TECHNOLOGY

Modern factories in the region specialize in the manufacture of high-tech goods. Singapore is a major center for printing. Skilled workers (above) use the latest technology to produce books, magazines, packaging, and other printed products for clients all over the world.

♦ *Companies from Japan, Europe, and the U.S.A. have opened plants and offices across South East Asia.*

Pineapple

Durian

Mango

Banana

Coconut

TROPICAL FRUIT

Many tropical fruits, such as pineapples, coconuts, bananas, and mangoes, are grown in the region. Indonesia and the Philippines grow over half the world's coconuts, and Thailand produces one-fifth of the world's pineapples. The durian is a large fruit, up to 8 in. (20 cm) across, with a hard, thorny husk and cream colored flesh.

♦ *Durians give off such a powerful smell that some airlines do not allow passengers to carry them aboard their airplanes.*

IRRIGATED RICE TERRACES

Rice has been the staple crop and traditional food of the region for thousands of years. There are many varieties of rice, each suited to different conditions of climate, soil, and altitude. In hilly areas, farmers grow rice on steep terraces, such as these on the island of Bali (right). The terraces are irrigated to keep the rice plants under water while they grow. In areas with less rainfall, other crops, such as cassava, a starchy, root plant, are grown.

♦ *Plant scientists crossbreed rice plants to produce improved varieties so that farmers can have two or more harvests a year.*

LOGGING

The forests that cover so much of this region contain valuable resources. Hardwood trees, such as teak, are prized for making furniture. Kapur trees are used for building houses. Trees also supply plywood, paper, and resin. After the trees have been cut, they are floated down rivers to mills on the coast, like these logs in Sarawak, Malaysia (above). Many countries have banned the export of logs in order to encourage their own factories to process them into wood and paper. Over-exploitation of the region's forests in some countries, such as Thailand and the Philippines, has caused great damage to the environment.

♦ *In 1997-98, forest fires swept across Borneo, Indonesia, endangering animals such as the orangutan.*

RUBBER-TAPPING

Natural rubber comes from the milky sap of trees that grow in tropical climates, such as Phuket island, in Thailand (below). Grooves, cut into the bark, channel the sap into containers secured to the trunk, where it is collected. This process is called rubber-tapping. The sticky substance is rolled into balls for delivery to the factory, where it is made into rubber.

♦ *Malaysia's many large rubber plantations produce half the world's natural rubber.*

Pitcher plant

MUDSKIPPERS

In the mangrove swamps around the Indian Ocean, strange fish, called mudskippers, cling to tree roots or lie on the mudflats. These fish have gills and can breathe under water but spend most of their time out of water. As long as they remain moist, mudskippers can stay alive by breathing air. They use their pelvic fins like legs to scamper across the muddy surface, eating algae, worms, and shrimp.

♦ *Mudskippers' eyes can swivel to give them all-around vision.*

Rafflesia

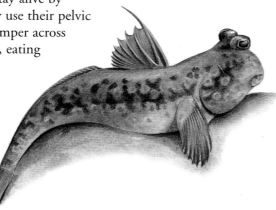

At its lowest, the **Turfan Depression** lies 505 ft. (154 m) below sea level.

China
and its neighbors
People and places

China is the world's third largest country and, with over a billion people, is the most populated country on Earth. It has one of the world's oldest civilizations, dating back about 5,000 years. Among the great inventions of the ancient Chinese were the compass, gunpowder, and the art of papermaking. Chinese religion, art, and architecture have had an important influence on the culture of its neighbors. In 1949, the government of China became communist, and today, China is the world's largest communist state. Korea remains divided into a communist northern state and a democratic southern state.

THE GREAT WALL

The continuous Great Wall of China was started in 221 B.C. and was built to defend the northern provinces from attack.
♦ **A force of 300,000 slaves built the stone wall.**

POTALA PALACE

This magnificent palace in Lhasa, Tibet, was built for the Dalai Lama, the country's spiritual ruler. Started in the 17th century, it was added to over the centuries until it had over 1,000 rooms. In 1950, China occupied Tibet and repressed Buddhism, forcing the Dalai Lama to leave in 1959. Today, Tibet is a self-governing region of China.
♦ **Lhasa was once called the Forbidden City because visitors were not allowed to enter the city.**

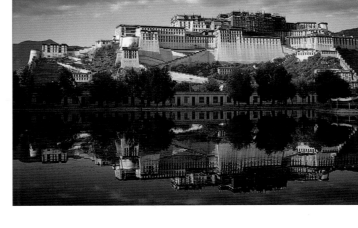

TERRACOTTA ARMY

In 1974, workers digging a well near Xi'an in China discovered 7,500 life-sized model soldiers made from terracotta. They were found in the tomb of the emperor Ch'in Shih Huang Ti (259–210 B.C.).
♦ **Xi'an was the ancient capital of the Han Chinese.**

DRAGON DANCE

To celebrate the Chinese New Year, people make huge paper dragons and carry them through the streets. Firecrackers are let off to frighten away evil spirits. The Chinese New Year marks the start of spring, and its date varies according to the phases of the moon. It can take place between January 21st and February 20th.
♦ **New Year is the Chinese people's most important holiday. Families get together to exchange gifts.**

Map labels:
KAZAKHSTAN
KYRGYZSTAN
TIEN SHAN
Ürümqi
Turf Depre
Kashi
Aksu
Tarim Basin
Takla Makan Desert
ALTUN
TAJIKISTAN
PAKISTAN
Hotan
KUNLUN
INDIA
PLATEAU
QING ZANG
OF TIBET
HIMALAYAS
NEPAL
Mt. Everest
Xigaze
Lha
BHUTAN

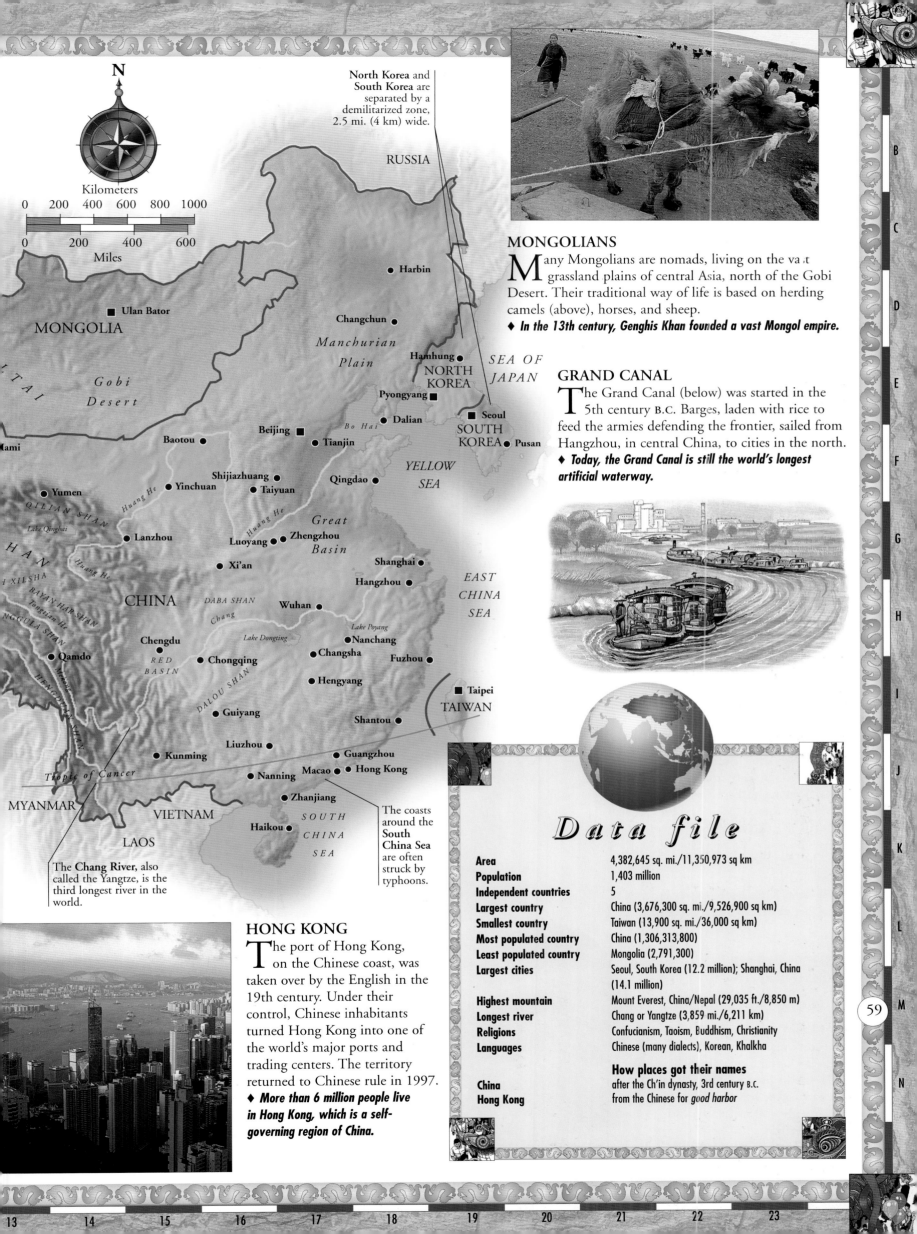

North Korea and South Korea are separated by a demilitarized zone, 2.5 mi. (4 km) wide.

Kilometers
0 200 400 600 800 1000

0 200 400 600
Miles

N

RUSSIA

Harbin

Ulan Bator

MONGOLIA

Changchun

Manchurian Plain

Hamhung

SEA OF JAPAN

NORTH KOREA

Pyongyang

Gobi Desert

Beijing

Dalian

Seoul

SOUTH KOREA

Pusan

Bo Hai

Baotou

Tianjin

YELLOW SEA

Yumen

Shijiazhuang

Yinchuan

Taiyuan

Qingdao

QILIAN SHAN

Huang He

Lake Qinghai

Lanzhou

Luoyang

Zhengzhou

Great Basin

Shanghai

Huang He

XILSHA

Xi'an

Hangzhou

EAST CHINA SEA

CHINA

DABA SHAN

Wuhan

Chang

BAYAN HAR SHAN

Tongtian He

NG GULA SHAN

Chengdu

RED BASIN

Chongqing

Lake Dongting

Lake Poyang

Nanchang

Changsha

Fuzhou

Qamdo

DALOU SHAN

Hengyang

HENGDUAN SHAN

Guiyang

Taipei

TAIWAN

Shantou

Liuzhou

Tropic of Cancer

Kunming

Guangzhou

MYANMAR

Nanning

Macao

Hong Kong

VIETNAM

Zhanjiang

SOUTH CHINA SEA

LAOS

Haikou

The coasts around the South China Sea are often struck by typhoons.

The Chang River, also called the Yangtze, is the third longest river in the world.

MONGOLIANS

Many Mongolians are nomads, living on the vast grassland plains of central Asia, north of the Gobi Desert. Their traditional way of life is based on herding camels (above), horses, and sheep.
♦ *In the 13th century, Genghis Khan founded a vast Mongol empire.*

GRAND CANAL

The Grand Canal (below) was started in the 5th century B.C. Barges, laden with rice to feed the armies defending the frontier, sailed from Hangzhou, in central China, to cities in the north.
♦ *Today, the Grand Canal is still the world's longest artificial waterway.*

HONG KONG

The port of Hong Kong, on the Chinese coast, was taken over by the English in the 19th century. Under their control, Chinese inhabitants turned Hong Kong into one of the world's major ports and trading centers. The territory returned to Chinese rule in 1997.
♦ *More than 6 million people live in Hong Kong, which is a self-governing region of China.*

Data file

Area	4,382,645 sq. mi./11,350,973 sq km
Population	1,403 million
Independent countries	5
Largest country	China (3,676,300 sq. mi./9,526,900 sq km)
Smallest country	Taiwan (13,900 sq. mi./36,000 sq km)
Most populated country	China (1,306,313,800)
Least populated country	Mongolia (2,791,300)
Largest cities	Seoul, South Korea (12.2 million); Shanghai, China (14.1 million)
Highest mountain	Mount Everest, China/Nepal (29,035 ft./8,850 m)
Longest river	Chang or Yangtze (3,859 mi./6,211 km)
Religions	Confucianism, Taoism, Buddhism, Christianity
Languages	Chinese (many dialects), Korean, Khalkha
	How places got their names
China	after the Ch'in dynasty, 3rd century B.C.
Hong Kong	from the Chinese for *good harbor*

China and its neighbors:
Nature, farming, and industry

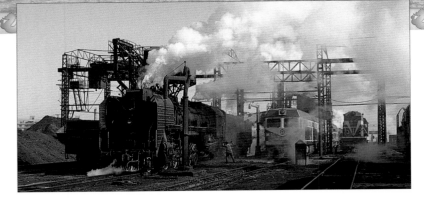

China's vast population lives mainly in the eastern third of the country and most of the region's people are farmers. The other two-thirds, and Mongolia, contain some of the world's most remote and inhospitable places. They include the Gobi and Takla Makan deserts, and the high, cold Tibetan plateau. In these areas, the traditional lifestyle is based on herding. China has vast mineral wealth, and large reserves of coal and oil. Factories in Taiwan, South Korea, and the Guangdong area of China make many of the toys, shoes, mobile phones, and other goods used by people all over the world.

STEAM LOCOMOTIVES

To carry passengers and heavy freight, such as coal, across China, the country has over 36,000 mi. (58,000 km) of railway. Over half of China's trains are still pulled by steam locomotives, such as this one (above) in Changchun. Most of the track is located in the crowded eastern regions, and only since the 1970s, have new lines been laid to the remote regions of the north and west.
◆ *Today, many of the more isolated Chinese settlements rely on airplanes.*

TAKLA MAKAN DESERT

The desert summers are very hot and the winters very cold. Rivers that run down from the mountains often dry up completely. Some hoofed animals, such as asses, gazelles, and antelopes, can live in the desert. Herds of wild asses, now less common than they once were, roam huge distances as they search for grass.
◆ *The wild ass, or onager, is a fast runner and can go for two or three days without drinking.*

Gazelle

Wild ass

Argali

LIMESTONE HILLS

The hills of Guilin, in southern China, are a famous natural wonder. They rise almost vertically from the rice fields around them and have been a popular subject of Chinese paintings since ancient times. The hills are made of limestone, which is easily worn away by rainwater. Over many years, erosion has left steep hills filled with caves.
◆ *The warm, fertile south produces two crops of rice a year and a third crop of vegetables.*

FISHING WITH CORMORANTS

On the river Li, in southern China, people use cormorants to catch fish. The birds dive under water to make their catch, but a ring around their throats prevents them from swallowing the fish. People go out at night and use lanterns to attract the fish.
◆ *Many Chinese villages have special ponds that are used for fish farming.*

SHIPYARDS

South Korea and Taiwan are two of the world's leaders in shipbuilding. Repairing ships is also an important industry in Taiwan. Ship-breakers take old vessels apart and recycle metal and other materials. For a small country, such as Taiwan, which has few natural resources of its own, recycling is a way of getting iron and steel for shipbuilding. It helps Taiwan compete with countries that can make ships with their own resources. This vessel (right) is in a dry dock at Kaohsiung, a deepwater port in Taiwan. The ship was placed on supports, the water drained out, and repairs were made.
◆ *South Korea's official name is the Republic of Korea. North Korea is called the Democratic People's Republic of Korea.*

CHINESE FOOD

In the south of China, people mostly eat rice, but in the north, they eat noodles, steamed buns, and bread, all made from wheat. The staple foods are served with a great variety of spicy sauces. This Kaili woman from Guizo (right) is hanging out noodles to dry.

♦ *Milk is taken from cattle, sheep, goats, and water buffalo.*

Red panda

ELECTRONICS

South Korea and Taiwan have built up their economies by specializing in making goods for export. They began with low-cost goods, such as pocket calculators and digital watches. Later, they developed advanced computer industries (below).

♦ *Many workers in the electronics factories are women.*

Musk deer

Bamboo

Giant panda

CHINA'S FARMING REGIONS

Only one-tenth of China's land is suitable for cultivation. Half of this is given over to rice paddy fields or irrigated for other crops, such as cabbages and carrots. Rice, the main crop, is grown mainly in the south. Almost one-third of China is pasture and is used for herding livestock, raised mainly for meat.

Sugarcane, mandarins, and pineapples grow in warm Guanxi province.

Guangdong is an important area for cabbages and carrots.

Melons and other fruit are grown in oases in the western deserts.

Yaks are raised on the high plateau of Tibet.

- Forest
- Herding
- Wheat, corn, & cotton
- Herding, wheat, corn, & cotton
- Rice (usually two crops a year)
- Mixed forest, rice, wheat, corn, & cotton

BAMBOO FOREST

The mountains of central China were once covered in huge areas of bamboo forest. Over the centuries, so much forest has been cut down that some animals, such as the giant panda, have become rare. Bamboo leaves and shoots are not very nutritious, so giant pandas spend two-thirds of their time eating.

♦ *Bamboo is a type of grass. It is the fastest-growing plant in the world.*

Golden pheasant

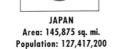

JAPAN
Area: 145,875 sq. mi.
Population: 127,417,200

Japan

Japan is made up of four large islands and four thousand smaller ones, lying between the northern Pacific Ocean and the mainland of Asia. It is a land of violent natural forces, with frequent earthquakes, over a hundred volcanoes, and fierce storms, called typhoons. It is also a country of great natural beauty with its mountains, forests, and famous gardens of cherry trees. Japan is a fascinating mixture of ancient and modern. There are thousands of Buddhist and Shinto shrines where religious festivals are held. After the devastation of World War II, Japan rebuilt itself to become one of the world's major industrial powers.

TOKYO, JAPAN'S CAPITAL

Tokyo and its suburbs are part of the largest built-up area in the world, where over 30 million people live. It is so big that people have to travel long distances in fast, packed commuter trains to get to work. Tokyo is famous for its giant department stores. The Ginza (above) is a popular shopping district.
♦ *Many of the world's large companies have offices in Tokyo. The city is also an important banking center.*

JAPANESE FOOD

A typical Japanese meal consists of rice, soup, called miso, made from soybeans, and a number of small side dishes, called kazu (right). Other favorite foods include raw fish, either on its own (called sashimi) or with rice (sushi). Japanese chefs present dishes with great skill and artistic feeling.
♦ *Fugu, or blowfish, is a great delicacy. It is so poisonous that it has to be cooked by specially trained chefs.*

RICE FARMING

So much of Japan is covered in mountains, forests, or areas of poor soil that there is very little farmland to feed the large population. Japanese farmers have learned how to grow enough rice for all the country on small plots of land. They grow new strains of rice that produce more food, and they use pesticides, fertilizers, and automated rice harvesters (above).
♦ *Most rice farmers work part time in factories and offices to subsidize their earnings.*

WORKING ROBOTS

Although Japan has few natural resources, it is one of the world's most successful manufacturing countries. Japanese automobile factories use specially designed robots for many jobs, such as welding (below) in the Nissan automobile factory near Tokyo.
♦ *Japan's factories make more automobiles and cameras than any other country.*

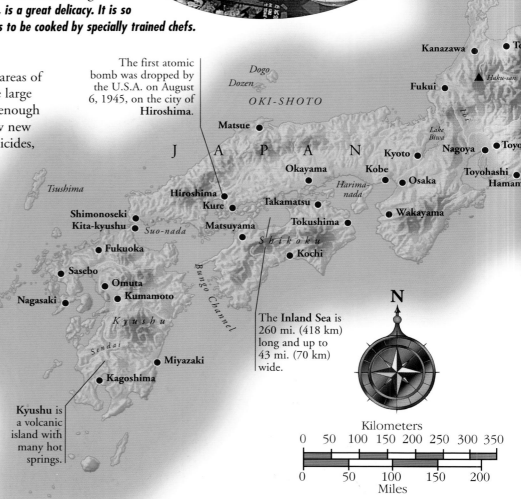

The first atomic bomb was dropped by the U.S.A. on August 6, 1945, on the city of **Hiroshima**.

SEA OF JAPAN

Suzu-misaki

Kanazawa   Toy

Dogo Dozen
OKI-SHOTO

Haku-san

Fukui

Matsue

Lake Biwa

J A P A N

Kyoto   Nagoya   Toyot

Okayama   Kobe   Toyohashi
Osaka   Hamam

Harima-nada

Hiroshima
Kure   Takamatsu

Shimonoseki   Matsuyama   Tokushima   Wakayama
Kita-kyushu   Suo-nada

Tsushima   Shikoku

Fukuoka   Kochi

Sasebo

Omuta
Nagasaki   Kumamoto

Kyushu

Sendai

The Inland Sea is 260 mi. (418 km) long and up to 43 mi. (70 km) wide.

Miyazaki

N

Kagoshima

Kyushu is a volcanic island with many hot springs.

Kilometers
0 50 100 150 200 250 300 350

0   50   100   150   200
Miles

The **Seikan Tunnel**, linking Hokkaido and Honshu islands, is the world's longest undersea tunnel (34 mi./54 km long).

KOBE EARTHQUAKE

Japan is located in a region where three of the giant plates which make up the earth's crust meet. When these plates move against each other, earthquakes occur. There are over 1,500 in Japan each year. In 1995, a severe earthquake destroyed the city of Kobe (right), killing 5,000 people.

♦ *The scientists who study and try to predict earthquakes are called seismologists.*

Honshu is the world's seventh largest island (87,806 sq. mi./ 227,415 sq km).

JAPANESE CHILDREN

These children (above right) are visiting the famous Yomeimon Gate at Toshoga shrine in Nikko. Japanese families are usually small, and children are greatly valued by their parents. Children receive lots of toys, and often have their own television and telephone. They are expected to work very hard at school. Many attend special classes to help them do better in exams and win a place at a top university.

♦ *In Japan, May 5 is a national holiday, called Children's Day.*

OFFSHORE AIRPORT

There is so little flat land in Japan that planners have to find new ways to make room for building. In Osaka Bay, they have built a whole airport on an artificial island 3 mi. (5 km) from the coast. Aircraft land and take off over the sea, so Kansai airport (below) can operate 24 hours a day without the noise disturbing anyone.

♦ *Tokyo's business districts have spread onto land reclaimed from the sea in Tokyo Bay.*

MACAQUES

Japanese macaques are found further north than any other monkey. They live in troops of up to 100 monkeys. They usually spend the day in trees eating leaves, but they are also good swimmers. In winter, they keep warm by bathing in hot springs (left). Macaques are very quick to learn new ways. One troop on Koshima Island taught each other how to wash their sweet potatoes before eating them.

♦ *Japanese macaques store their food in their cheeks.*

Data file

Area	145,875 sq. mi./377,815 sq km
Population	127 million
Capital city	Tokyo
Largest cities	Tokyo (12 million), Yokohama (3.6 million), Osaka (2.6 million)
Highest mountain	Mount Fuji (12,388 ft./3,776 m)
Longest river	Shinano (229 mi./368 km)
Largest lake	Biwa (260 sq. mi./674 sq km)
Religions	Shintoism, Buddhism
Currency	1 yen = 100 sen
	How places got their names
Hokkaido	from the Japanese for *northern land*
Honshu	from the Japanese for *chief island*
Tokyo	from the Japanese for *eastern capital*

Map labels:
Asahikawa
Asahi dake
Otaru · Sapporo · Obihiro · Kushiro
Hokkaido
Ishikari
Muroran
Hakodate
Tsugaru Strait
Aomori
Hirosaki · Hachinohe
Akita
Honshu
Sakata
Yamagata · Sendai
Niigata · Fukushima
Koriyama
Iwaki
Utsunomiya · Hitachi
Takasaki · Mito
Kasumiga-ura
Tokyo · Chiba
Kawasaki · Yokohama
Mt. Fuji · Yokosuka
Shizuoka
PACIFIC OCEAN

ALGERIA — Area: 919,595 sq. mi. Population: 32,531,900
ANGOLA — Area: 481,354 sq. mi. Population: 11,190,800
BENIN — Area: 43,450 sq. mi. Population: 7,460,000
BOTSWANA — Area: 224,607 sq. mi. Population: 1,640,100
BURKINA FASO — Area: 105,869 sq. mi. Population: 13,925,300
BURUNDI — Area: 10,026 sq. mi. Population: 6,370,600
CAMEROON — Area: 178,963 sq. mi. Population: 16,380,000
CAPE VERDE — Area: 1,557 sq. mi. Population: 418,200
CENTRAL AFRICAN REPUBLIC — Area: 240,324 sq. mi. Population: 3,799,900

Africa
People and places

Situated on both sides of the Equator, the huge, hot continent of Africa contains a fifth of the world's land area and is the second largest continent. It is the home of hundreds of tribes of native peoples, each with its own culture, beliefs, and languages. There are more than 250 types of native peoples in Nigeria alone. In north Africa, Arabic is the common language, and Islam is the main religion. In West Africa, farming and logging are important industries. South Africa, with its vast mineral deposits, is the wealthiest of the southern countries. In many of the 53 countries of Africa, civil wars and unstable governments cause great hardship to the people.

The **Sahara Desert** is the world's largest desert. Temperatures can be hotter than 120° F (50° C).

Statue of Liberty 300 ft. (91.5 m)

Great Pyramid 482 ft. (147 m)

Sydney Opera House 221 ft. (67.4 m)

Lake Volta, which is 3,275 sq. mi. (8,482 sq km), is the world's largest artificial lake.

THE GREAT RIFT VALLEY

A series of valleys, called the Great Rift Valley, extends for 3,750 mi. (6,000 km) all the way from the Red Sea to Mozambique. It appeared many years ago, when the land slipped down between huge cracks, called faults, in the earth's crust.

◆ *Parts of the Great Rift Valley have become deep lakes, such as Lake Nyasa in Malawi.*

MASAI PEOPLE

The Masai are cattle herders. They live on the grasslands of Kenya and Tanzania. Men may have several wives. Women and girls shave their heads and wear elaborate bead neckbands.

◆ *The Masai diet includes milk and blood from their cattle.*

LIFE IN THE VILLAGE

Many Africans live in traditional village homes built from earth, wood, grass, and sometimes animal skins. Other houses are built from bricks and have thatched roofs made of grass or reeds, such as these in Zimbabwe (above).

◆ *Village huts are sometimes grouped together inside a fence, or stockade, which also holds cattle, goats, and chickens.*

The **Cape of Good Hope** is often swept by terrible storms.

Kilometers
0 200 400 600 800 1000

0   200   400   600
Miles

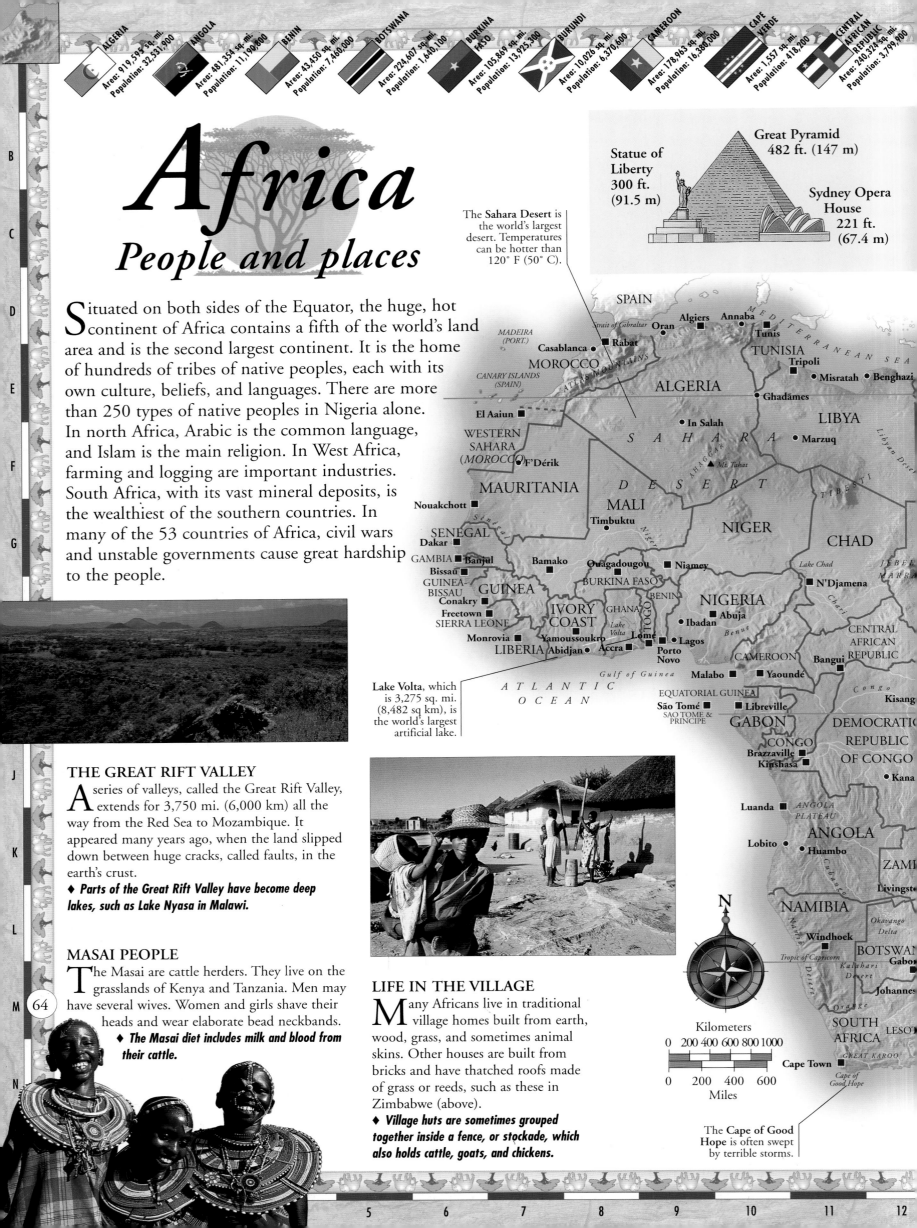

CHAD Area: 496,000 sq. mi. Population: 9,826,400	COMOROS Area: 719 sq. mi. Population: 671,200	CONGO Area: 132,047 sq. mi. Population: 3,039,100	DEMOCRATIC REPUBLIC OF CONGO Area: 905,446 sq. mi. Population: 60,085,800	DJIBOUTI Area: 8,950 sq. mi. Population: 476,700	EGYPT Area: 385,229 sq. mi. Population: 77,505,800	EQUATORIAL GUINEA Area: 10,830 sq. mi. Population: 535,900	ERITREA Area: 46,842 sq. mi. Population: 4,561,600	ETHIOPIA Area: 433,789 sq. mi. Population: 73,053,300

EGYPT'S PYRAMIDS

Pyramids are enormous, four-sided tombs that were built to hold the mummified bodies of Egyptian kings and queens. The biggest is the Great Pyramid at Giza, which was built about 2500 B.C.

♦ **The Great Pyramid is made from more than 2 million blocks of limestone.**

The **Suez Canal** is a vital waterway for ships traveling from Europe to Asia. It connects the Mediterranean Sea to the Red Sea.

The **Nile River,** which is 4,125 mi. (6,670 km) long, is the world's longest river.

AFRICAN MUSIC

Music is important in the lives of the African peoples. The extraordinary rhythms and lively sounds of traditional African music are often produced on drums and stringed instruments made from gourds, animal skins, and horns.

♦ **This musical instrument is used in Gambia, Africa's smallest mainland country.**

AFRICA'S LARGEST CITY

Cairo (above) is Egypt's capital and Africa's largest city. Like many African cities, it is bustling and filled with traffic. The minarets, or towers, of over 400 mosques rise above the packed bazaars of the old quarter. The modern section of the city is filled with office blocks, banks, and hotels.

♦ **Cairo's mixed population includes people from many different backgrounds and religions, such as Muslims, Coptic Christians, Jews, Turks, Europeans, and black Africans.**

NOMADIC WAY OF LIFE

The Tuaregs are a nomadic people who roam the Sahara Desert with their animals, searching for water and fresh pastures. Most nomads ride camels, although today some may use trucks.

♦ **About half a million people live a nomadic life in and around the Sahara Desert.**

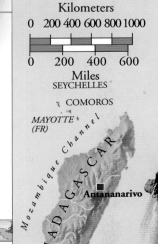

Map labels

Alexandria
Suez
Tropic of Cancer
EGYPT
Aswan
Lake Nasser
SAUDI ARABIA
Nubian Desert
Port Sudan
Atbara
Kassala
ERITREA
Asmera
YEMEN
Wad Medani
Gulf of Aden
El Obeid
Lake Tana
DJIBOUTI
Djibouti
Berbera
SUDAN
Addis Ababa
SOMALIA
ETHIOPIAN HIGHLANDS
White Nile
ETHIOPIA
UGANDA
Kampala
KENYA
Mogadishu
Kisumu
Equator
Mt. Kenya
RWANDA
Lake Victoria
Nairobi
Kismaayo
Kigali
INDIAN
BURUNDI
Kilimanjaro
Mombasa
Bujumbura
OCEAN
Dodoma
Zanzibar
Dar-es-Salaam
Lake Tanganyika
TANZANIA
Lake Nyasa
MALAWI
Lilongwe
Moçambique
Blantyre
Harare
MOZAMBIQUE
Beira
ZIMBABWE
Bulawayo
Limpopo
Maputo
SWAZILAND
Durban

Scale

Kilometers
0 200 400 600 800 1000

0 200 400 600
Miles
SEYCHELLES
COMOROS
MAYOTTE (FR)
Mozambique Channel
MADAGASCAR
Antananarivo

Data file

Area	11,512,708 sq. mi./29,817,713 sq km
Population	856 million
Independent countries	53, and 3 dependencies
Largest country	Sudan (966,757 sq. mi./2,503,890 sq km)
Smallest country	Seychelles (175 sq. mi./453 sq km)
Most populated country	Nigeria (128,772,000)
Least populated country	Seychelles (81,190)
Largest cities	Lagos, Nigeria (13.5 million); Cairo, Egypt (10.8 million)
Highest mountain	Kilimanjaro, Tanzania (19,340 ft./5,895 m)
Longest river	Nile (4,160mi./6,695 km)
Largest lake	Victoria (26,834 sq. mi./69,500 sq km)
Religions	Christian, Ethiopian Orthodox, Hindu, Muslim, local religions
Languages	Hundreds of native languages

How places got their names

Benin, Ghana, Mali	from early African empires
Chad	from Lake Chad
Gambia, Nigeria	from African rivers
Ivory Coast	from ivory, the tusks of elephants, which was traded there
Namibia	from the Namib Desert
Sierra Leone	from the Portuguese for *lion mountain*

65

GABON
Area: 103,347 sq. mi.
Population: 1,389,200

GAMBIA
Area: 4,127 sq. mi.
Population: 1,593,300

GHANA
Area: 92,098 sq. mi.
Population: 21,029,900

GUINEA
Area: 94,926 sq. mi.
Population: 9,467,900

GUINEA-BISSAU
Area: 13,948 sq. mi.
Population: 1,416,000

IVORY COAST
Area: 123,847 sq. mi.
Population: 18,142,000

KENYA
Area: 220,625 sq. mi.
Population: 33,829,600

LESOTHO
Area: 11,720 sq. mi.
Population: 1,867,000

LIBERIA
Area: 38,250 sq. mi.
Population: 3,482,200

Africa: *Nature*

Vast areas of unspoiled wilderness are found all across Africa, from the huge Sahara Desert in the north to the Kalahari and Namib deserts in the far south. Gorillas, giant forest pigs, monkeys, and countless birds live in the dense tropical rain forests of western and central Africa. Coral reefs are found in the warm waters off the east coast. Vast stretches of savannah grassland are home to giraffes, rhinos, and lions. Africa also has snowcapped volcanic mountains, rushing rivers, and huge lakes. The world's fastest land animal, the cheetah, and the world's largest land animal, the African elephant, are both found on this continent.

DESERT PLANTS

Many African plants are adapted to drought. Watermelons store water in their stems, while the welwitschia plant of the Namib Desert has a massive taproot that sucks up moisture deep beneath the desert's surface.

♦ *The welwitschia may live for as long as 2,000 years.*

Watermelon

Welwitschia

MIGRATION

Millions of wildebeest (above) live on the plains of northern Tanzania and southern Kenya. In this region, the rains come only at certain seasons. Vast herds of wildebeest follow the rains to find the best grazing land. On their journey, they cross from Tanzania's Serengeti National Park into Kenya by swimming across the Mara River.

♦ *More than 2 million wildebeest cross the Mara River each year.*

African elephant and calf

Thomson's gazelle

Leopard

LIBYA — Area: 678,400 sq. mi. Population: 5,765,600
MADAGASCAR — Area: 226,658 sq. mi. Population: 18,040,300
MALAWI — Area: 36,400 sq. mi. Population: 12,158,900
MALI — Area: 478,841 sq. mi. Population: 12,291,500
MAURITANIA — Area: 389,000 sq. mi. Population: 3,086,990
MAURITIUS — Area: 788 sq. mi. Population: 1,230,600
MOROCCO — Area: 177,117 sq. mi. Population: 32,725,800
MOZAMBIQUE — Area: 308,642 sq. mi. Population: 19,406,700
NAMIBIA — Area: 317,818 sq. mi. Population: 2,030,700

BAOBAB TREE

The tropical African baobab tree (right) has a wide trunk in which it stores water. The swollen trunk helps the tree survive the dry season.

♦ **The baobab is also called a bottle tree.**

SAVANNAH

Snowcapped Mount Kilimanjaro, in Tanzania, rises above a vast expanse of savannah grassland that stretches as far as the eye can see. Vast herds of grazing mammals, such as elephants, giraffes, buffaloes, zebras, and Thomson's gazelles feed on the savannah grasses. These grazing animals are hunted by predators, such as cheetahs, leopards, and lions.

♦ **The giraffe is the tallest animal in the world. It can grow up to 20 ft. (6 m) tall.**

Zebra   Buffalo   Giraffe

PROTECTED AREAS

Throughout Africa, there are national parks and reserves that protect habitats and wildlife of the continent. These parks stop people from hunting the animals and keep whole environments intact and safe.

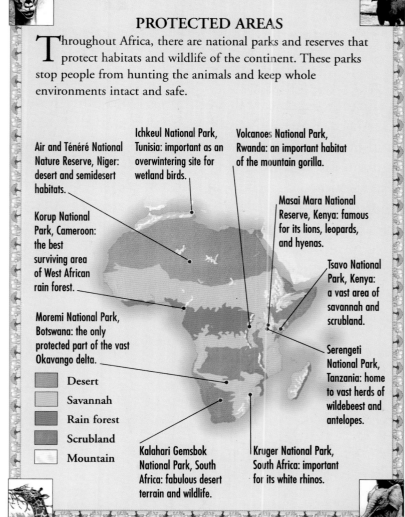

Air and Ténéré National Nature Reserve, Niger: desert and semidesert habitats.

Ichkeul National Park, Tunisia: important as an overwintering site for wetland birds.

Volcanoes National Park, Rwanda: an important habitat of the mountain gorilla.

Korup National Park, Cameroon: the best surviving area of West African rain forest.

Masai Mara National Reserve, Kenya: famous for its lions, leopards, and hyenas.

Moremi National Park, Botswana: the only protected part of the vast Okavango delta.

Tsavo National Park, Kenya: a vast area of savannah and scrubland.

Serengeti National Park, Tanzania: home to vast herds of wildebeest and antelopes.

- Desert
- Savannah
- Rain forest
- Scrubland
- Mountain

Kalahari Gemsbok National Park, South Africa: fabulous desert terrain and wildlife.

Kruger National Park, South Africa: important for its white rhinos.

LIFE IN THE DESERTS

Lack of water is the main problem faced by desert animals. In some areas, rain may not fall for years at a time. Many desert animals, such as camels, can go without water for long periods. Others, such as desert vipers and lizards, burrow in the sand to escape the intense heat of the sun and come out at night to search for food. Fennec foxes have large ears that let heat escape from their body.

♦ **Ostriches live in semidesert areas of the Kalahari and Namib deserts.**

Fennec fox   Arabian camel   Ostrich   Lizard   Desert viper

RIVERS AND LAKES

Africa has many mighty rivers, such as the Nile, the Congo, and the Zambezi. There are spectacular waterfalls, too, such as Victoria Falls, and many shimmering lakes, which are breeding grounds for flamingoes. Many of Africa's rivers and lakes are a year-round supply of water for the animals that come to drink each day. Other lakes and rivers are seasonal and are dry for most of the year. Hippos and crocodiles (left) spend most of their time in the water. Hippos come onto land only after sunset to graze, and female crocodiles lay their eggs in hollows on the riverbanks.

♦ **The female Nile crocodile may lay as many as 80 eggs in one batch.**

NIGER
Area: 458,075 sq. mi.
Population: 11,665,900

NIGERIA
Area: 356,669 sq. mi.
Population: 128,772,000

RWANDA
Area: 10,169 sq. mi.
Population: 8,440,800

SÃO TOMÉ AND PRINCIPE
Area: 386 sq. mi.
Population: 187,400

SENEGAL
Area: 75,955 sq. mi.
Population: 11,126,800

SEYCHELLES
Area: 175 sq. mi.
Population: 81,190

SIERRA LEONE
Area: 27,699 sq. mi.
Population: 6,017,600

SOMALIA
Area: 246,201 sq. mi.
Population: 8,591,600

SOUTH AFRICA
Area: 473,290 sq. mi.
Population: 44,344,100

Africa:
Farming and industry

Africa has a great wealth of mineral and other resources. South Africa, Algeria, Namibia, Zambia, and the Democratic Republic of Congo are major suppliers of copper, gold, diamonds, uranium, oil, and natural gas to the rest of the world. Mining for these resources, especially in southern Africa, is the most important industry. Many countries in western Africa, as well as Egypt and Kenya, earn money by exporting dates, cotton, tea, coffee, peanuts, and palm oil. For many Africans, farming to feed themselves remains the main economic activity. They mostly use traditional tools and methods to grow crops and herd livestock.

TRADITIONAL FARMING

Most African families practice "subsistence" farming using traditional methods (above). They grow enough food for their family, and there may be a little left for sale at market.
♦ **Staple crops include corn, millet, rice, sorghum, bananas, cassava, and sweet potatoes.**

VINEYARDS

The dry, warm summers and mild winters of South Africa's climate are ideal for growing grapes, which are used to make wine. Grapevines (above) were first planted in South Africa by Dutch settlers in the mid-1700s. Today there are over 386 sq. mi. (1,000 sq km) of vineyards stretching inland from Cape Town.
♦ **South Africa's commercial farmers grow sugar cane, citrus fruits, and cotton, as well as grapes, for export.**

MARKET DAY

Colorful market scenes, such as this one in Sudan (right), are common throughout Africa. Markets are an important meeting place. People come to sell any surplus vegetables and fruit they have grown, and to exchange news. In many African countries, the market produce is grown and sold by the women of the family. Women also make handmade items, such as decorated earthenware pots, hand-printed fabrics, and colorful clothes to sell at market.
♦ **The island of Zanzibar, off the coast of Tanzania, produces most of the world's cloves, a strong spice used in cooking all over the world.**

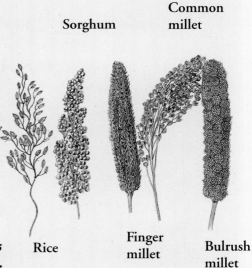

HERDING LIVESTOCK

Today, people from many different African nations still herd cattle, goats, sheep, and camels in much the same way their ancestors did. They allow their livestock to graze on any available grassland, and, during the dry season, often travel long distances with their animals looking for new grazing land. This young Masai herder (below) is leading his cattle to new pastures in Kenya.
♦ *In arid regions, women and children often walk some distance to collect water.*

GRAIN CROPS

Grains, such as millet and sorghum, are grown widely throughout central Africa. Finger millet is rich in minerals and can be stored for up to five years. Bulrush millet resists drought. Millet is usually eaten as porridge, while sorghum is ground and made into bread. Rice is grown in countries such as Egypt and Mali, where rivers are used for irrigation.
♦ **Potatoes, tomatoes, and eggplants are an important addition to the diet.**

Sorghum

Common millet

Rice

Finger millet

Bulrush millet

SUDAN	SWAZILAND	TANZANIA	TOGO	TUNISIA	UGANDA	ZAMBIA	ZIMBABWE
Area: 966,757 sq. mi. Population: 40,187,500	Area: 6,704 sq. mi. Population: 1,173,900	Area: 342,081 sq. mi. Population: 36,766,400	Area: 21,925 sq. mi. Population: 5,681,500	Area: 59,664 sq. mi. Population: 10,075,000	Area: 76,080 sq. mi. Population: 27,269,500	Area: 290,586 sq. mi. Population: 11,261,800	Area: 150,873 sq. mi. Population: 12,747,000

HANDICRAFTS

Colorful handicrafts are made throughout Africa. They are sold for local use as well as to tourists. Morocco is famous for its boldly patterned, hand-knotted carpets and rugs (left). They are hung up for display in narrow-laned markets, called souks. Other African handicrafts include leather bags, shoes, hand-printed clothes, pottery, woven mats and baskets, brassware, and carved wooden animals and masks.

♦ *In Lesotho, southern Africa, goats' mohair is a vital export both as yarn and in finely woven materials.*

INDUSTRY AND AGRICULTURE

This map shows the main agricultural areas and some of the main areas where mineral resources and fossil fuels have been found. The most heavily industrialized mining areas are in South Africa, Zimbabwe, the Democratic Republic of Congo, and Zambia. These areas have vast deposits of gold, diamonds, copper, platinum, uranium, and chrome ore. Oil and natural gas are plentiful north of the Sahara, in Libya, Algeria, and Egypt.

Nigeria has huge reserves of iron ore and coal, but its main export is oil.

Copper makes up 80 percent of the Democratic Republic of Congo's export industry.

Egypt extracts high-grade iron ore, which is processed into iron and steel.

Burundi has the world's richest deposits of vanadium, used to make steel alloys.

△ Diamonds
△ Iron ore
▲ Coal
▲ Oil
△ Gold
△ Copper
△ Other minerals
○ Fruit and vegetables
○ Arable and grazing

Mining for diamonds and gold is the main activity in South Africa.

RICH IN MINERALS

Africans have mined and processed minerals, including gold, for over 2,000 years. South Africa has the richest deposits of valuable minerals. Using modern technology, today's miners are able to drill for gold and diamonds (below) deep underground.

♦ *The gold mine at Carletonville, South Africa, is the world's deepest mine. It stretches 12,392 ft. (3,777 m) underground.*

SUGAR FACTORY

Sudan, the largest country in Africa, has the biggest sugar factory on the continent and the third largest in the world, at Kanana (below). Raw sugar is made from the sweet sap of sugar cane, a giant grass that grows up to 15 ft. (4.5 m) tall. The sap is processed into sugar crystals at the factory. Other important African crops grown for sale and export include most of the world's palm kernels, 75 percent of the world's palm oil and cocoa, and 30 percent of its high-quality cotton.

♦ *Egypt produces more dates than any other country.*

AUSTRALIA Area: 2,966,200 sq. mi. Population: 20,090,400
FIJI Area: 7,056 sq. mi. Population: 893,100
KIRIBATI Area: 328 sq. mi. Population: 103,100
MARSHALL ISLANDS Area: 70 sq. mi. Population: 59,070
MICRONESIA Area: 271 sq. mi. Population: 108,100
NAURU Area: 8 sq. mi. Population: 13,050
NEW ZEALAND Area: 103,788 sq. mi. Population: 4,035,500
SOLOMON ISLANDS Area: 10,954 sq. mi. Population: 538,000
TONGA Area: 301 sq. mi. Population: 112,400

Australia and Oceania
People and places

This continent includes Australia, New Zealand, and thousands of small islands scattered across the Pacific Ocean. Australia has an area over 20 times bigger than all the other countries of this continent put together, and almost three-quarters of the region's people live there. Most Australians live near the southeast coast. Aborigines are Australia's original inhabitants and have lived there for thousands of years. Maoris were the first people in New Zealand, sailing from the Polynesian islands in about A.D. 800. Both these peoples are now minorities in countries where the majority are descended from European settlers.

ABORIGINES

Aborigines adapted to a dry land. They learned where to find water and food and hunted wild animals with spears and boomerangs. In a dance called a corroboree (left), they celebrate their ancestral spirits.

♦ *In recent years, Aborigines have regained control over some of the lands that were taken from them by the European settlers.*

ULURU

Uluru, the Aborigines' name for Ayer's Rock, is an ancient block of sandstone in Australia's Northern Territory. It rises 1,142 ft. (348 m) above the desert plain, and glows red, pink, and purple in the setting sun. To the Aborigines, Uluru is a sacred place, where many of the paths taken by their ancestral spirits meet. There are Aboriginal paintings in the caves at the rock's base.

♦ *In 1985, Uluru was returned to the local Aboriginal people, who now manage it as a national park with the Australian government.*

SYDNEY HARBOR

Sydney is Australia's oldest city. It was founded in 1788, when the first European settlers made use of its superb natural harbor. Two of the country's most famous landmarks, the Opera House and the Harbor Bridge (above), are in Sydney.

♦ *The unique roofs of the Sydney Opera House, which opened in 1973, were designed to look like giant sails.*

ARAFURA SEA
TIMOR SEA
Melville I.
INDIAN OCEAN
Darwin
Arnhem Land
Gulf of Carpentar
Daly
Roper

Darwin was almost completely destroyed by a cyclone on Christmas Day, 1974.

Wyndham
Derby
Kimberley Plateau
Fitzroy
Barkly Tableland
Georgina

Port Hedland
Great Sandy Desert
NORTHERN TERRITORY

Fortescue
▲ Mt. Bruce
Tropic of Capricorn
Gibson Desert
MACDONNELL RANGES
Alice Springs

Carnarvon
Murchison
WESTERN AUSTRALIA
▲ Uluru
Simpson Desert

SOUTH AUSTRALIA
L. Ey

Great Victoria Desert
L. Everard
L. Torr

Kalgoorlie
Nullarbor Plain
L. Gairdner

Perth
Fremantle
Great Australian Bight
N
Adelaide

Albany
Kangaroo I.

The longest straight section of railway track in the world crosses the **Nullarbor Plain**. It is 297 mi. (478 km) long!

Kilometers
0 200 400 600 800 1000

0 200 400 600
Miles

FLYING DOCTOR SERVICE

Australians in remote settlements live far away from doctors and hospitals. To deal with this problem, the Royal Flying Doctor Service was founded in 1928. With 38 aircraft, the service provides emergency medical care across a vast area.

♦ *People use radio to contact a flying doctor for medical help.*

TUVALU
Area: 9 sq. mi.
Population: 11,640

VANUATU
Area: 5,699 sq. mi.
Population: 205,800

SAMOA
Area: 1,093 sq. mi.
Population: 177,300

MOUNTAINTOPS

Many Pacific islands are the peaks of underwater mountains. Others, such as Bora Bora (right), are extinct volcanoes fringed by beautiful lagoons and coral reefs.

♦ *Bora Bora covers just 6 sq. mi. (15 sq km) and is home to 2,000 people. They are Polynesians who speak Tahitian.*

Data file

Area	3,104,725 sq. mi./8,041,183 sq km
Population	26 million
Independent countries	12, and 9 dependencies
Largest country	Australia (2,966,200 sq. mi./7,682,300 sq km)
Smallest country	Nauru (8 sq. mi./21 sq km)
Most populated country	Australia (20,090,400)
Least populated country	Tuvalu (11,640)
Largest cities	Sydney, Australia (4.3 million), Melbourne, Australia (3.8 million)
Highest mountain	Mount Cook, New Zealand (12,316 ft./3,764 m)
Longest river	Murray–Darling, Australia (2,330 mi./3,780 km)
Largest lake	Eyre, Australia (3,598 sq. mi./9,320 sq km)
Largest desert	Great Sandy, Australia (130,695 sq. mi./338,500 sq km)
Religions	Protestant, Roman Catholic
Languages	English, French, Maori, Samoan, and native languages

How places got their names

New Zealand	after the Dutch province of Zeeland
Polynesia	from the Greek for *many islands*
Samoa	named by Maoris after the moa, a giant bird that is now extinct

SPORTING NATIONS

Australians and New Zealanders are keen sports fans and flock to international games (above). Cricket and rugby are favorite summer games.

♦ *The famous New Zealand rugby team is known as the All Blacks.*

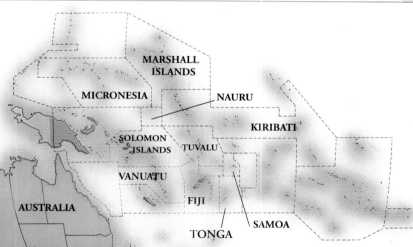

MARSHALL ISLANDS

MICRONESIA

NAURU

KIRIBATI

SOLOMON ISLANDS

TUVALU

VANUATU

AUSTRALIA

FIJI

SAMOA

TONGA

PACIFIC ISLANDS

People from South East Asia traveled to the Pacific islands in canoes about 5,000 years ago and settled there. The islanders developed hundreds of cultures and languages, but they all traded with each other. There are three main groups of Pacific peoples: Polynesians, Melanesians, and Micronesians. During the 19th century, many of the islands became colonies of France, Britain, and the United States, and the islanders converted to the Christian religion.

♦ *Most Pacific countries are made up of many islands. Kiribati has 33 small islands, which are spread out over 1.2 million sq. mi. (3 million sq km) of ocean.*

Map labels

Cape York

Great Barrier Reef

Cairns

CORAL SEA

Townsville

Rockhampton

Fraser I.

QUEENSLAND

Brisbane

NEW SOUTH WALES

GREAT DIVIDING RANGE

Darling

Lachlan

Newcastle

Sydney

Canberra   Wollongong

AUSTRALIAN CAPITAL TERRITORY

Murray

PACIFIC OCEAN

VICTORIA

Mt. Kosciusko

Ballarat   Melbourne

Geelong

King I.   Bass Strait   Flinders I.

TASMAN SEA

Launceston

TASMANIA

Hobart

New Zealand's capital, **Wellington**, is the most southern capital city in the world.

Auckland

Hamilton

North Island

L. Taupo

NEW ZEALAND

South Island

Wellington

SOUTHERN ALPS

Mt. Cook

Christchurch

Stewart I.

The Australian island state of **Tasmania** gets its name from the Dutch explorer, Abel Tasman, who sighted the island in 1642.

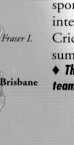

MAORI MASK

Many Maoris still live in tribal villages. They keep up their arts of tattooing and intricate wood carving, such as this mask (left).

♦ *Maoris call New Zealand Aotearoa, meaning "land of the long white cloud."*

71

Australia and Oceania: *Nature*

The land mass of Australia is ancient. It has been separated from other continents for a very long time. The wind and rain have worked on its rocks and mountains for so long that they have worn away, making Australia the flattest continent. Central Australia is an area of deserts of sand and stone; however, the southeast is wetter. Over many years, the region's isolation has led to the development of a number of unique species of plants and animals. Over a hundred kinds of marsupials are found in Australia. There are also unusual egg-laying mammals, such as the echidna and duck-billed platypus. New Zealand has an incredible variety of landscapes, such as mountains, glaciers, hot springs, rain forests, and grasslands. The country is home to unusual flightless birds, such as the kiwi.

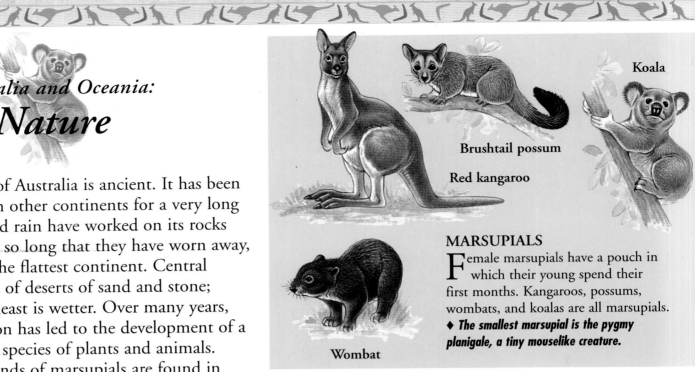

Koala

Brushtail possum

Red kangaroo

Wombat

MARSUPIALS

Female marsupials have a pouch in which their young spend their first months. Kangaroos, possums, wombats, and koalas are all marsupials.
♦ *The smallest marsupial is the pygmy planigale, a tiny mouselike creature.*

FLIGHTLESS BIRDS

The largest flightless bird in Australia is the emu. New Zealand's flightless birds are smaller. The kiwi (right) is New Zealand's national bird. It has long feathers that look like fur.
♦ *The flightless takahe was thought to be extinct until it was rediscovered in 1948.*

Gould's monitor lizard

Dingo

Termite mound

Thorny devil

Sturt's desert pea

Spinifex pigeon

IN THE OUTBACK

The outback is bush land that covers two-thirds of Australia. It is very dry, although there are some swamps and rivers. Droughts are common, but when it does rain, the outback blooms with colorful flowers, and birds appear in great numbers. Plants and animals must adapt to the lack of water. Spinifex grass has a wide system of roots to draw in moisture. Sturt's desert pea has tiny hairs on its leaves to reduce water loss in the heat. Gould's monitor lizard escapes the heat in its underground burrow.
♦ *The thorny devil is a lizard that lives in sand and scrub. At night, it absorbs dew through its skin.*

TASMANIAN WOLF

The Tasmanian wolf, or thylacine, is thought to be extinct, but every year people claim to have seen its paw marks in the remote woods of Tasmania. The wolf was a marsupial with a doglike head, and it barked and growled like a dog. It hunted at night, either alone or in pairs, feeding on wallabies, rats, and birds. The last captive animal died in the 1930s.

♦ *Tasmanian wolves were hunted by humans because they attacked sheep and chickens.*

Hammerhead shark

Tiger shark

EUCALYPTUS FOREST

Eucalyptuses, or gum trees, were unique to Australia. Today, they are grown all over the world in gardens and commercial forests. There are hundreds of kinds, some towering like these trees in Cathedral Range State Park (above), and others that are small bushes.

♦ *Koalas live in gum trees and eat the young shoots and leaves.*

GREAT BARRIER REEF

Off the coast of northeast Australia lies the largest living structure in the world: the Great Barrier Reef. It is made up of over 2,000 individual coral reefs spread along 1,300 mi. (2,100 km). Reefs are made over thousands of years from the skeletons of tiny sea creatures, called coral polyps, that attach themselves to rocks. When corals die, new ones grow on top.

♦ *The waters around the reef are filled with sharks and other fish.*

Nurse shark

Spinner shark

Parrotfish

Thresher shark

Australia and Oceania:
Farming and industry

The wealth of Australia and New Zealand is based on farming and mining. Both countries export a great deal of farm produce, such as wool, beef, lamb, and dairy products. Australia has large reserves of metals and minerals, and Australians use modern roads to get them to ports where they are shipped to the world's markets. The Pacific islands have far fewer natural resources, and many islands are so small that they have little farmland. Fishing and increasing tourism help their economies.

TONGAN CRAFT

This woman from the island of Tonga is painting tapa cloth made from the bark of mulberry trees. Other traditional crafts on the islands are basket-making, mat-weaving, and beadwork. The Tongan people are Polynesians. Most work as farmers, growing coconuts, bananas, and cassava, or raising cattle, poultry, and pigs. Fishing is also important.

♦ Coconut oil is used to make soap and cosmetics.

MINING

Australia has large deposits of minerals and metals. There is coal on the east coast and iron ore (left) in Western Australia. Coober Pedy, in South Australia, has the world's largest opal mine. Gold, diamonds, and silver are found in other parts of the country. Many mines, such as Mount Isa in Queensland, are in harsh, dry regions, and miners work under extremely tough conditions.

♦ **The tiny island of Nauru has deposits of phosphates, used to make fertilizers. New Caledonia has valuable reserves of nickel.**

CULTURED PEARLS

French Polynesia, a group of islands belonging to France, and Australia are two of the world's leading centers of pearl farming. Pearls are made by oysters when a grain of sand lodges inside the shell and the oyster coats the grain with a hard substance called nacre. The Japanese discovered how to make cultured pearls by placing a speck of oyster shell inside the oyster. The oyster is returned to the sea bed, and after about two years, a pearl has formed.

♦ **Polynesia specializes in black pearls, but the most sought-after pearls are perfectly round and white.**

GEOTHERMAL POWER

The Rotorua district of New Zealand's North Island is a volcanic region steaming with hot springs, mud pools, and geysers. Water beneath the earth's surface is heated by hot volcanic rocks and rises under pressure. New Zealand has pioneered the use of this geothermal energy to produce electricity, which is used to heat homes in winter and power refrigeration units in summer. Rising steam is channeled by pipes to drive turbines. The first power plant was built at Wairakei (left). New Zealand produces about 8 percent of its electricity this way.

♦ *At Whakarewarewa, there are over 500 hot springs. Some of the water bubbles up in mud pools or forms geysers that blast water 100 ft. (30 m) into the air.*

ROAD TRAIN

In a country as vast as Australia, goods have to be taken great distances along rough roads from farms and mines to markets and ports. Outside built-up areas, drivers sometimes attach two or three long trailers to a single truck, making a road train.

♦ *The distance from Sydney to Darwin is over 2,485 mi. (4,000 km). Only one major road runs across central Australia, passing through the town of Alice Springs.*

KIWI FRUIT

New Zealand's farmers grow exotic fruits, such as the Chinese gooseberry or kiwi fruit. These are grown on small farms (left).

♦ *Tamarillos, nashis, and passion fruit are also grown in New Zealand.*

MODERN SYDNEY

The state capital of New South Wales, Sydney (left), is Australia's biggest city, its main port, and its most important center for manufacturing. Sydney has become the center of Australian banking, and most of the country's largest companies have their head offices there. Many large Japanese companies also have branches in Sydney.

♦ *In Sydney, you can ride by monorail from the business district to Darling Harbor, a waterfront shopping and entertainment center.*

SHEEP FARMING

Sheep and cattle farming are big business in Australia and New Zealand. Australian sheep ranches are huge, and farmers use trucks to drive around and feed the animals. Australia is the world's biggest exporter of wool.

♦ *After refrigerators became available in the 1880s, Australia and New Zealand were able to export meat and other foods to the rest of the world.*

The Arctic

HUSKY SLEDS

Before motorized snowmobiles were invented, the easiest way for people to cross the frozen Arctic wastes was by sleds pulled by huskies. These strong dogs come originally from northern Siberia. They have thick coats to keep out the cold and can pull loads up to twice their own weight. They are usually harnessed together into teams of at least six, with one husky as the lead dog. In parts of Greenland, husky sleds are still the main means of transport.

♦ ***Racing sleds with teams of huskies is a popular sport in Alaska and northern Canada.***

The Arctic is the cold region around the North Pole. It consists of a large ocean — almost surrounded by land — that is always partly frozen. In winter, the frozen area gets bigger, and the sun barely appears above the horizon. In summer, some of the ice melts, and ships can pass through the Arctic waters. Greenland, the world's largest island, is almost entirely covered by a massive ice cap up to 1.9 mi. (3 km) thick. Greenland's average temperature is -27° F (-33° C). Animals, such as polar bears and foxes, can survive the bitter cold, and the Arctic seas are rich in fish and whales. For centuries, the Inuit have lived in the Arctic, hunting and fishing.

ICEBREAKER

When the Arctic Ocean freezes in winter, ordinary ships cannot get through. Special icebreakers with reinforced hulls and very powerful engines, such as this one (left) belonging to the Russian navy, are used to crush the ice and keep the Arctic waterways open.

♦ ***At the North Pole, in the center of the Arctic region, the seas are permanently frozen.***

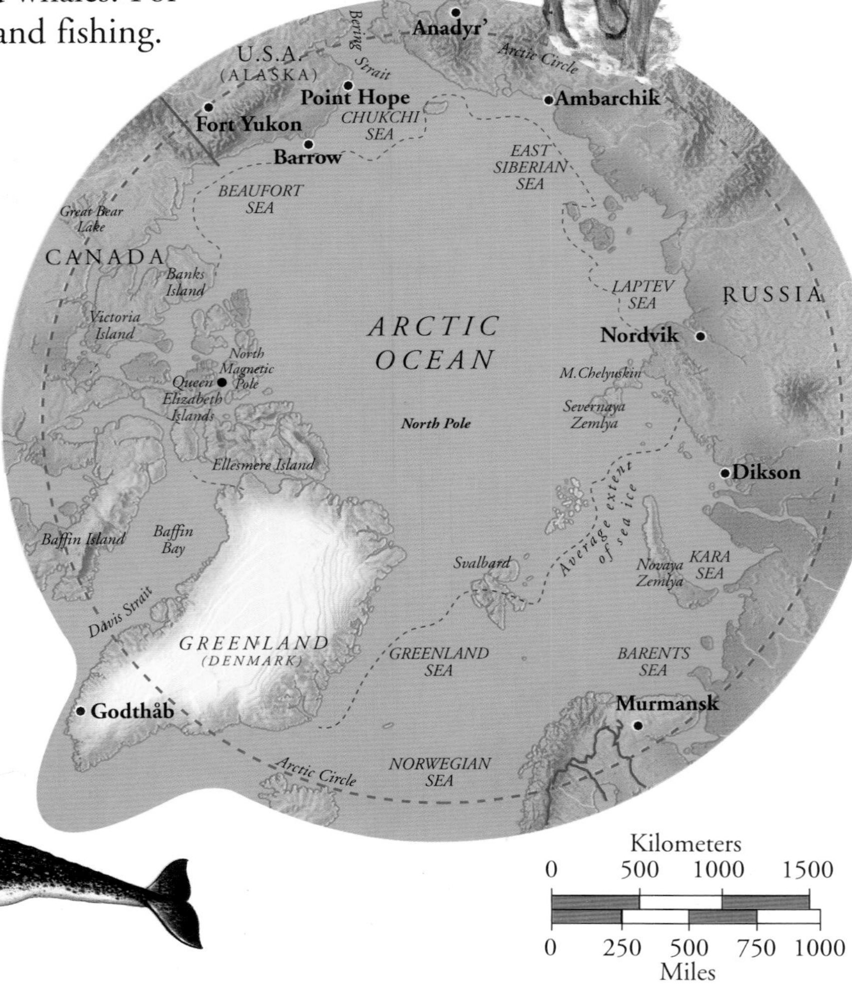

Anadyr'
Bering Strait
Arctic Circle
U.S.A. (ALASKA)
Point Hope
Ambarchik
Fort Yukon
CHUKCHI SEA
Barrow
EAST SIBERIAN SEA
BEAUFORT SEA
Great Bear Lake
CANADA
Banks Island
LAPTEV SEA
RUSSIA
Victoria Island
ARCTIC OCEAN
Nordvik
North Magnetic Pole
Queen Elizabeth Islands
M.Chelyuskin
Severnaya Zemlya
North Pole
Ellesmere Island
Dikson
Baffin Island
Baffin Bay
Average extent of sea ice
Svalbard
Novaya Zemlya
KARA SEA
Davis Strait
GREENLAND (DENMARK)
GREENLAND SEA
BARENTS SEA
Godthåb
Murmansk
Arctic Circle
NORWEGIAN SEA
Kilometers
0 500 1000 1500
0 250 500 750 1000
Miles

WHALES

Although they live in the sea, whales are mammals. They must come to the surface regularly to breathe air. Females give birth to live young and feed them with their own milk. Many kinds of whales live in the Arctic waters, where they feed on fish and tiny sea creatures, called krill. Some whales move south to warmer waters to breed.

♦ ***The male narwhal has a long, spiraling tusk up to 8 ft. (2.5 m) long that it uses as a jousting weapon when competing for females.***

Narwhal

Beluga whale and calf

Humpback whale

GREENLANDERS

Most of the people of Greenland live in coastal settlements, where the ice melts for some of the year. The largest town is the capital, Godthåb (right), which has over 13,000 inhabitants. Greenlanders belong to two groups, the native Inuit and Danish settlers.

♦ ***Greenland is a self-governing province of Denmark.***

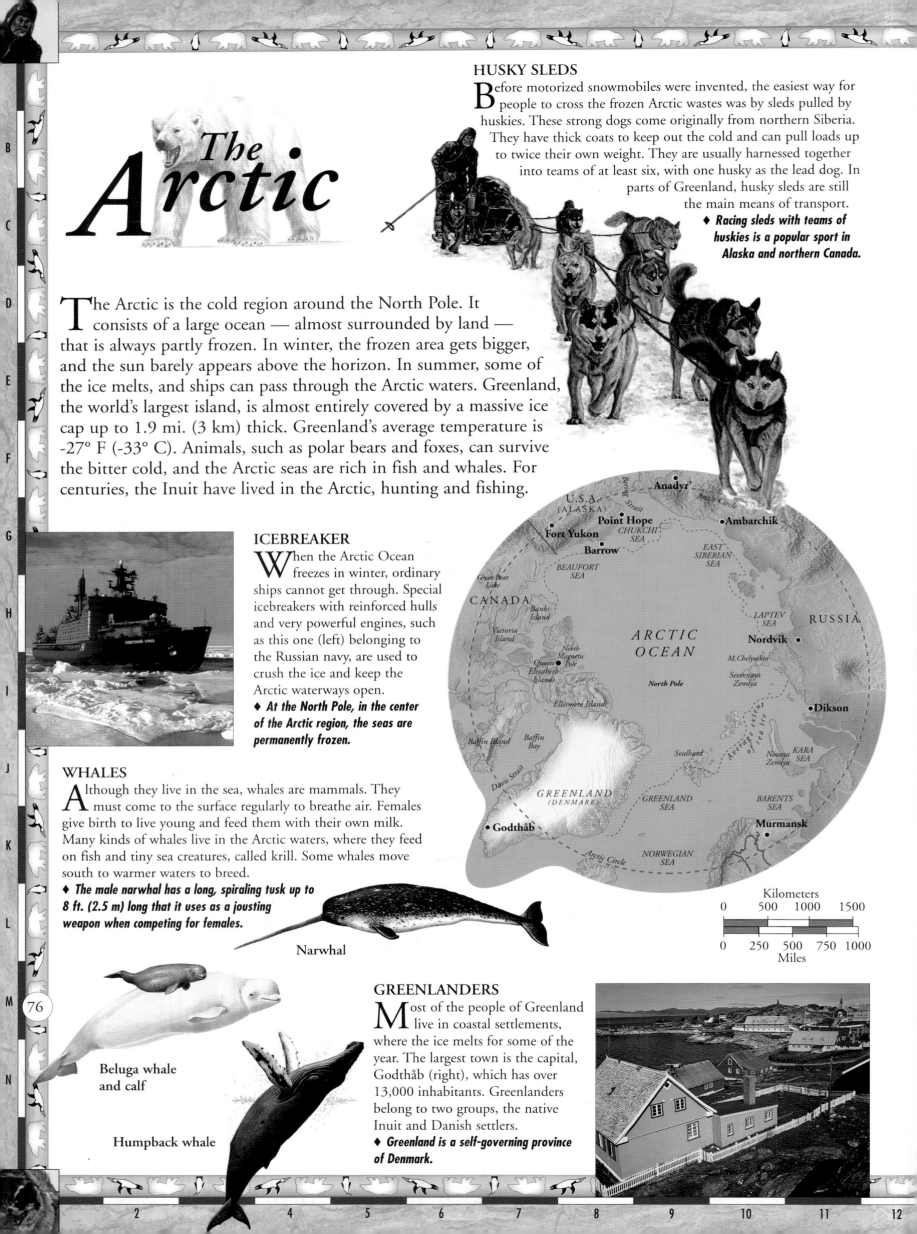

Antarctica

Antarctica is the frozen continent that surrounds the South Pole. A giant ice cap covers the land. Beneath the ice lie mountains and valleys. In winter, temperatures drop to -58° F (-50° C), and fierce winds blow from the high ground. In 1911, the Norwegian explorer Roald Amundsen and his team became the first people to reach the South Pole.

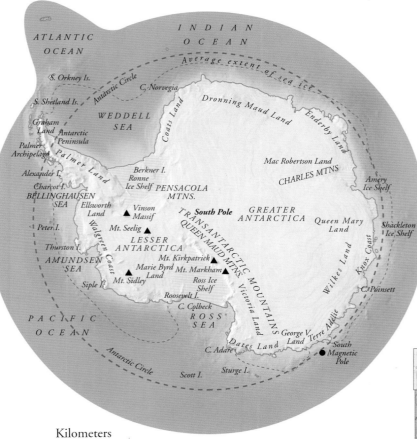

Kilometers
0   500   1000   1500

0   250   500   750 1000
Miles

AMUNDSEN-SCOTT STATION

No one lives permanently in Antarctica, but many countries have scientific bases there. The U.S. Amundsen-Scott station (below) lies at the South Pole. Scientists at the bases extract ice samples from deep inside the ice cap to investigate how the earth's climate has changed over thousands of years.

♦ *British explorer Robert Scott led the second group to reach the South Pole. He died on the way back.*

ICEBERGS

Icebergs are found in both the Arctic and Antarctic. They are huge chunks of ice, which break off from ice sheets or glaciers that meet the sea. Ocean currents can move them great distances into warmer water, where they can be a danger to shipping.

♦ *Over 90 percent of an iceberg's mass is below the ocean's surface.*

PENGUINS

Penguins are found along the coasts of Antarctica and in the surrounding oceans. These gentoo penguins (right) nest in huge colonies called rookeries on the Antarctic peninsula and South Georgia. The penguins make nests from stones, and lay two eggs. For a month, the parents take turns incubating the eggs. When the chicks hatch, they huddle together for safety from predators.

♦ *Emperor penguins, the largest species, can be up to 3 ft. (1 m) tall.*

LICHENS

Lichens (left) grow where no other living things can survive, including high Antarctic mountains. They cling to bare rock surfaces, growing by tiny amounts each year. Some lichens can live for 4,000 years.

♦ *Lichens are living partnerships between fungi and algae.*

Data file

Area of the Arctic Ocean	5,108,000 sq. mi./13,230,000 sq km
Area of Antarctica	5,500,000 sq. mi./14,245,000 sq km
Highest mountain	Vinson Massif, Antarctica (16,863 ft./5,140 m)
Longest glacier	Lambert Glacier, Antarctica (435 mi./700 km)
Largest lake	Great Bear, Arctic Canada (12,096 sq. mi./ 31,328 sq km)
Countries above the Arctic Circle	Greenland (Denmark), Canada, U.S.A. (Alaska), Russia, Finland, Sweden, Norway
Countries with bases in Antarctica	U.S.A., Russia, United Kingdom, Argentina, Australia, Chile, France, India, New Zealand
	How places got their names
Antarctica	means opposite the Arctic
Arctic	from the Greek for "bear"
Greenland	named by the Vikings, who found grass near the shore

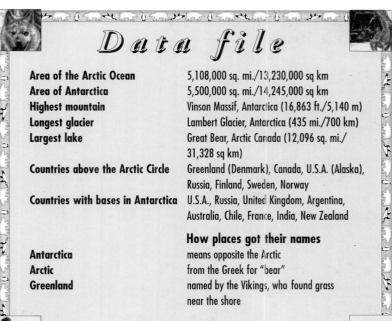

Index and Gazetteer

In this index and gazetteer, page numbers refer to a text entry in the book. If the page number is prefixed by ≈, there is also a picture of the subject. Places shown on the maps have a page number followed by a grid reference (e.g., **Banks Island** 76 H7). Turn to the page (76), then use your finger to trace a line from the letter (H) across the page. Trace another line from the number (7) up the page. Where the two points meet, you will find the place on the map.

Abbreviations for countries controlling dependencies:

DK.	Denmark
FR.	France
EC.	Ecuador
INDIA	India
NETH.	Netherlands
N.Z.	New Zealand
PORT.	Portugal
SP.	Spain
U.K.	United Kingdom
U.S.	United States of America

79